Look Again

IN BALTIMORE

Look Again
IN BALTIMORE

TEXT BY

John Dorsey

PHOTOGRAPHY BY

James DuSel

For Ana Maciel and Robert Armacost

This book has been brought to publication through the generous assistance of Robert W. Armacost and of John Dorsey's friends from his college years at Harvard: Walter William Birge III, Perry D. Caminis, Robert M. Coen, Robert S. Feinberg, Samuel B. Hopkins, and Andrew G. Kotsatos.

The Johns Hopkins University Press
2715 North Charles Street
Baltimore, Maryland 21218-4363
www.press.jhu.edu

Library of Congress Cataloging-in-Publication Data

Dorsey, John R., 1938–
   Look again in Baltimore / John Dorsey ; photography by James DuSel.
      p.   cm.
   ISBN 0-8018-7415-7 (hardcover : alk. paper)
   1. Architecture—Maryland—Baltimore—Pictorial works. 2. Baltimore (Maryland)—Buildings, structures, etc.—Pictorial works. 3. Architecture—Themes, motives. 4. Baltimore (Maryland)—Description and travel.   I. DuSel, James. II. Title.
   NA735.B3D675 2005
   975.2'6'00222—dc22   2005000737

A catalog record for this book is available from the British Library.

Contents

Liberty of thought is the life of the soul.

Voltaire

Curiosity is one of the permanent and certain characteristics of a vigorous mind.

Samuel Johnson

It is through Art, and through Art only,
that we can realize our perfection; through Art and Art
only that we can shield ourselves from the sordid perils
of actual existence.

Oscar Wilde

> Men grind and grind in the mill of a truism, and nothing comes out but what was put in. But the moment they desert the tradition for a spontaneous thought, then poetry, wit, hope, virtue, learning, anecdote, all flock to their aid.

Ralph Waldo Emerson

To criticize is to appreciate, to appropriate, to take intellectual possession, to establish in fine a relation with the criticized thing and to make it one's own.

Henry James

The work never is done while the power to work remains ... To live is to function. That is all there is in living.

Oliver Wendell Holmes

I think, therefore I am.

René Descartes

Introduction

To UNDERSTAND THE PURPOSE of this book, it might help to know how it came about. Shortly after I retired in 1999 from the job of *Baltimore Sun* art critic, I got a call from James DuSel. He had exhibited his photography locally for several years. I had seen it, admired it, and written a few—too few—words about it. He had quite properly never communicated while I was in a position to notice his work in print, but now he called and got right to the point.

"Would you consider doing a book with me?" he asked.

"Yes," I said, without a second's hesitation. After all, my principal interests were art and architecture, and he was a photographer who took unusual pictures of architecture. Not façades, but details, aspects—a corner of a building, a cut-off portico, a wall with a vine sprawling over it, the apse end of a church, parts of columns. Important and unimportant buildings: the Baltimore Museum of Art, the Mitchell Courthouse, a shoe repair shop, a carriage house, a transit waiting shed, the Basilica of the Assumption. Mostly exteriors but a few interiors—a grand staircase, an empty bedroom. And occasionally not even architecture—a sculpture, a tied-up curtain beside a mess of electrical conduits.

No matter what the image, the pictures I had seen were beautifully produced, with subtle lighting, rich tonalities, and clarity of details, and above all they were thought provoking. Sometimes they made you slap your forehead and think, "My God, I've seen that building a hundred times, but I never noticed *that* before." So often they caught the essence of a building or an aspect of architecture that a more inclusive picture would have missed. Sometimes they seemed quirky—why take a picture of a knotted curtain?—but none was ever boring, and the quirky ones could generate unexpected thought patterns. The photographer behind them obviously had a creative and incisive mind, and I was both flattered that he wanted to talk about doing a book together and eager to find out what he would propose.

As it turned out, his proposal was totally general and completely lacked specifics; that brilliant reserve produced this book. He brought me a generous assemblage of prints and several books related to the history of photography. There is no record of the conversation we had, so I do not quote verbatim, but he said something like, "John, I want you to look at these photographs and write whatever you think." We decided that first day on only one arbitrary limit: pictures had to have been taken in Baltimore City. That narrowed the field from Jim's entire output to a manageable number to choose from (somewhat more than a hundred images) and established identifiable geographical parameters. Otherwise there were no guidelines, in terms of order of choice, what to look for in any particular image, whether to favor content over style or vice versa, or any limitations of subject matter. With any image chosen to think about, my mind could go wherever it wanted to, and it did—resulting over time in a wide spectrum of responses to the individual images.

Sometimes the focus was on the specific building pictured. Sometimes it was on an aspect of the history of architecture. Sometimes it was about the photograph as a photograph or about photography and its history in a more general way. And sometimes the picture stimulated quite different thoughts—about art, history, literature, social questions, even personal and family memories.

Inevitably, however, as the book's combination of images and texts developed, certain emphases emerged to give it thematic form based on the similarity of our interests and concerns. We're both interested in architecture, in Baltimore, and in aesthetic felicity. Those interests combine to produce a concern for the urban environment—a somewhat high-falutin' way of saying what we see around us in the city—and a desire to encourage the same concern in as many others as possible. To have that, however, it is necessary for people not just to look, but to see, and to think about what they see. So an even more basic theme of the book is the importance of seeing and thinking. These and related interests gradually combined to produce a fourfold structure of related themes, which interweave and support one another.

1. to encourage people to look at architecture in a new way both in this book and around them in the world—to focus and concentrate on it, and thus learn to appreciate it to a greater and more meaningful degree. Jim's images are ideal for that purpose, for architecture seen in detail can stimulate a response and create a relationship between viewer and object better than architecture seen as a whole.

Because of the ubiquity of architecture, because whether inside or outside we are continuously surrounded by it, it tends to become subject to what Jim calls "the anesthesia of daily life." He explains: "As we rush to and fro, our concentration on daily business acts as a pair of blinders which, among other things, relegates the built environment to a series of anonymous blobs on the horizon of consciousness. As a result, we ignore the very things by which our civilization will be remembered." Even if we do not totally ignore them all the time, we tend at most to glance at the buildings we pass, mentally pigeonhole them in terms of type of structure—house, church, store—and in terms of style—column/classical, pointed arch/Gothic—and that's that.

This book is intended to act as a re-verse set of blinders, analogous to Jim's own experience as a photographer. "I work with a large view camera, and when I put the dark cloth over my head and focus on the image, it blinders out immediate concerns and allows me to see everything that I normally blinder out when I'm living my daily life."

For people to notice, it is necessary not to take pictures of façades as a whole because people will think, "Oh, I know that," and then pay as little mind as when they see the building in passing. To catch the viewer's attention, Jim focuses on a detail or portion and encourages thought about that focus—how the architect dealt with a small part; put together mass and void, structure and ornament; whether it was done gracefully or clumsily, and so on. It is hoped that the viewer, having been induced to focus on that part, will pay more attention when next seeing the building as a whole. Appreciation of the detail leads to appreciation of the whole and to paying more attention in general, which Jim describes as one of the major goals of his photography: "I want the print to be seductive, I want it to be somewhat mesmerizing. Sure, it's partly because I feel complimented when somebody says, 'This looks better than the real thing.' But on the other hand, the real thing that I want people to do is look at the real thing."

2. to encourage people, as a result of seeing herein architecture both fine and humble plus occasional nonarchitectural details (a sculpture, a shadow), to pay attention to the urban environment of Baltimore and, by extension, of cities in general. Appreciation of that environment will deepen understanding of the necessity of doing as much as possible to enhance it.

Architecture books tend to include only the significant. There is significant architecture herein, to be sure, but much else as well—a garage, former waterworks valve houses, a modest group of rowhouses, a suburban porch corner, and so on. They are all part of the visual vocabulary of the city.

When, some years ago, the west side of Baltimore's downtown became a renewal area, many people were mystified by preservationists' objections to plans to tear down buildings that were not major examples of architecture. Those buildings were, however, part of the context, and they needed to remain in order for the context to remain. We hope this book will help people to pay attention to context.

Not everything can or should be preserved, of course, and it's important to know what shouldn't as well as what should. That's one of the goals of Jim's work. "Really, I like people to rediscover what it is to see," he says, "or to discover that, if they never did. Because I think if people could rediscover what it is to see, among other things they wouldn't put up with the ugliness that pervades the world—strip malls, etc., etc., etc." Getting rid of the bad is just as important as keeping the good. And doing both will enhance the urban environment more than doing one and not the other.

3. in addition to their relevance to architecture and the urban environment, these photographs have resonance on other levels. They can show that what enters our daily lives connects us with the tapestry of civilization and makes us a part of it. Equally, they can provoke thoughts on social and cultural aspects of civilization, contemporary and otherwise. A photograph of the interior of the building that now houses Whole Foods supermarket in Mount Washington, but taken several years ago when it was empty, shows its architecture to be essentially a basilica form, which descends from ancient times. We buy our broccoli in a building that's based on the Basilica of Trajan in Rome

(A.D. 98–112) and the Church of San Francesco in Ravenna (560).

An empty niche on the front of the Baltimore Museum of Art leads to thoughts of how the United States has failed to fulfill its obligations as the richest and most powerful nation on Earth. A stairway in an Italian Renaissance Revival building at the Maryland Institute College of Art not only recalls the Italians' fascination with the stairway, going back to Piranesi, Bernini, and beyond, but leads as well to thoughts of how the lofty ideals and goals of student days all too often become compromised by the realities of life. A close-up of a cannon mouth recalls an image in Alfred Stieglitz's eighty-one-photograph "portrait" of Georgia O'Keeffe and, as such, connects this largely unnoticed object, as photographed, with the history of photography and of modernism.

These photographs show us that we are, in fact, connected to everything if we only take the time and effort to think of the connections. And such an effort is more than worth its cost, for it makes us conscious of the richness of life.

4. but there is another reason for that kind of thought, and that is as an end in itself. We hope this combination of images and texts will lead the viewer-reader to a sense of how the experience of art can stimulate original thought, which is at once the deepest purpose of art and the greatest joy of life.

This book is a marriage of the photographer's art and the critic's response to it. And the critic's responsibility, through that response, is not to attempt to hand down the truth, but to bring the art and the viewer together in such a way as to stimulate the viewer's own thought processes.

One reason for the critic's habitual reiteration in one form or another that "I represent only one opinion" is the genuine desire not to be seen as the voice of authority, because such a perception on the part of the reader tends to close rather than open thought. The proper function of the critic is to make the reader think, not to prevent him from thinking by giving him the idea that his thinking has been done for him.

To perform that function as a critic, I tried to write about my own response to art, not on the basis of some theoretical background but on how it related to me—to my emotions, to how I saw the world, to something with which the reader might be able to identify, at least enough to think at some level, even if unconsciously, "Okay, if he can relate to that work, maybe I can, too"—and then go do it.

Stimulating creative, original thought on the part of the viewer-reader is equally important to Jim and me. That's probably because in terms of the functions that brought us together to collaborate on this book—that is, as photographer and critic—we are largely autodidacts.

We both went to college, and Jim to graduate school, but I majored in history and he in classics. He has never had outside training in photography, nor I in criticism. I did have one course in art history and one in architecture history, but they were survey courses stretching from ancient times to yesterday—you know the sort of thing, look out the window and you miss the French Renaissance. Essentially, our training has come from reading, seeing, and practicing.

Believe it or not, that's not to pat us on the back, but to point out why independent thought is so important to us and why we think it's important for everyone. As Jim puts it, in terms of shooting a photograph, "I have a picture in my mind of what I want. I don't always achieve it, and then that's phenomenally frustrating." In terms of mastering darkroom techniques, he says, "I screwed up and tried again and again. Sometimes I'd come close to tears because it just would not work." In terms of his approach to photography overall, he says, "I just kept at it. I guess I'm just very persevering and very stubborn. I wanted to figure it out on my own."

And he did.

To understand his work better, it helps to know something about his style, how it relates to the history of photography, in particular architectural photography, and how his techniques, processes, and materials support the style.

James DuSel's photography, though it reflects multiple influences, is of course the product of his unique vision. While Jim is deeply versed in the history of his art and especially interested in nine-teenth-century French photography, his vision also owes a debt to American art and abstract art. Were he not aware of artists such as Walker Evans and Dorothea Lange, he would be less likely to take a picture of an empty bedroom and make it a paean to the working class. Were he not aware of artists such as Charles Sheeler, Alfred Stieglitz, Morris Louis, and Mark Rothko, he would be less likely to produce works that manifestly relate to the language of modernism. But there is a period and a style of architectural photography to which his work in this book is most closely linked.

In *Architecture Transformed,* a his-tory of architectural photography, co-author Cervin Robinson identifies two styles of the genre: factual and experiential. The factual imparts infor-mation, in what the photographer pre-sumably thinks of as an objective way. The factual photograph shows as much of the building as possible, as clearly as possible, to give the viewer the greatest amount of information. Essentially, it

is a quantitative approach. The experi-ential, on the other hand, is qualitative and more subjective. It shows not the whole building or whole façade but a segment that attempts to communicate to the viewer the essence or spirit of the work of architecture. Experiential photography of architecture is less in-formative than factual photography but more insightful. It puts the viewer in a personal relationship with the building by showing what it is like to experi-ence part of it up close and by showing where the photographer was placed in relation to the building.

Of a 1923 photograph by Arthur Köster of architect Erich Mendelsohn's Einstein Tower, Robinson writes, "To make the building's message single-minded, a fragment is shown, where a more complete view could have dissi-pated the picture's impact . . . The pic-ture has proved significant . . . in part because it summed up the building's spirit in a way that other, more general views did not" (*Architecture Trans-formed,* 1987, p. 92).

DuSel is not solely an architectural photographer, but when photographing architecture he clearly fits the experien-tial category. He photographs elements of architecture that often sum up the building's spirit, even when they don't show part of what one sees in the usual view of it. An excellent example is the photograph of a small portion of the exterior of the basement floor of the Baltimore Museum of Art. Although the photo shows an extremely minor segment of the building, the perfect relationship of all parts of the segment indicates architect John Russell Pope's qualities—his thorough academic training, his refined aesthetic sensibility, and his attention to the smallest details—in a way that a view of the portico would not. One would expect a good architect to make an impressive portico, but the greatness of the architect is even more apparent when he can take an out-of-the-way bit of basement and make its proportions so fine as to be thrilling.

DuSel achieves that summary quality time after time. His photograph of a tiny corner of the entrance to Evergreen clearly shows the house's grandeur. His shot of a dormer interior, bathed in light, at a Boys' Latin School building indicates architect Lawrence Hall Fowler's ability, like that of Pope, to be pleasing down to the details. His picture of the transit waiting shed at Falls and Edgevale roads emphasizes the Arts

and Crafts aspects of the design. His view of the side of St. John's Church, Huntingdon, makes it look more like the nineteenth-century Ecclesiological movement's idea of country church architecture—the spirit in which St. John's was built—than would a view of the more imposing front.

DuSel can summarize the essence of a building by showing what it is and what it isn't in the same photograph. The photo of the ornamentation on a doorway of Mount Vernon Place United Methodist Church indicates the church's appeal to Babbittry. Praise of this building as a great work of architecture, rather than as an engaging piece of Victorian Gothic Revival, is a classic example of the provincial tendency to glorify the respectable. Elsewhere, DuSel corrects Charles E. Cassell's attempt at the Richardsonian Romanesque style in the Greek Orthodox Cathedral by showing a portion of the building arranged asymmetrically, in the Richardsonian manner, whereas Cassell got the master's vision wrong by designing a symmetrical façade.

As Robinson points out, the factual style came to the fore in the 1880s and the experiential style advanced after

1890. Two of its practitioners were Eugene Atget and Frederick Evans, both of whom DuSel regards as influences on his work. DuSel thinks of Atget—who is most famous for recording the old Paris of his time in thousands of pictures of streetscapes and details of architecture—as the single most important model for his work.

"Atget rarely documents a building the way that photographers of the 1880s would do in that magisterial style," DuSel says, "but rather he gives vignettes of buildings that in fact do document, not the whole but rather the part. He produced basically a catalogue of details, and that's the kind of thing that has had a great deal of resonance with me."

Another similarity between Atget and DuSel is that each has taken a large number of pictures in his city of residence, Paris and Baltimore, respectively, and the work of each concentrates on a period before his lifetime. Atget (1857–1927) practiced photography from the 1890s to the 1920s, but as the catalogue of the exhibit "Photography and Architecture: 1839–1939" (1982) states, "[Atget] photographed in a highly selective fashion, avoiding almost all works of the nineteenth century, for example … On the other hand,

seventeenth- and eighteenth-century architecture interested him greatly" (p. 260). DuSel photographs buildings a little closer to his own time but still before it. He was born in 1950, has been concentrating steadily on photography since the early 1980s, and photographs nineteenth- and early-twentieth-century Baltimore architecture, very little after 1930.

A few years ago he made a trip to Spain to photograph Romanesque architecture, indicating an interest in the distant past that he shares with Evans (1853–1943), the famous English photographer of Gothic cathedrals. More than subject matter, however, DuSel feels a debt to Evans "in terms of approach, composition, and a cussed intransigence about getting the results that you want."

In approach, DuSel terms Evans "contemplative." In terms of composition, Robinson writes that Evans "eliminates all that is inessential" (*Architecture Transformed*, 1987, p. 78). Both of those are certainly characteristics of DuSel's images, and we will just have to take his word that he shares Evans's "cussed intransigence." His work, at any rate, looks as if he gets the results that he wants.

DuSel also mentions one other precedent for his work, French architectural photography of the 1850s, the period when architectural photography first came into its own, which, he says, "has been a certain construct and model for me." He points out that "viewpoints are almost constantly a surprise" and also that photographers of the period are perceptive and communicating about what he calls the "mood" of a building.

DuSel's viewpoints are a surprise in terms of what parts of respected architecture he takes—the bottom of a doorway at Clarence M. Mitchell, Jr. Courthouse; the exterior of the back of First Unitarian Church; a corner of the portico at Mount Clare. He also surprises by what examples of unheralded architecture he usually chooses. Once in a while they are what one might expect, gems that he wants to put forward, such as the apartment building at 4300 Roland Avenue. But more often they are obscure bits and pieces of the urban scene, modest storefronts, the substructure of a bridge, a wall of a shoe repair shop facing a side street that is in effect an alley.

As to "mood," we have everything from the mourning sculpture at Green Mount Cemetery, taken on a day that looks as if the sky is about to weep, to the fun one finds in the bunched-up eclecticism DuSel captures at the former Temple Oheb Shalom, to the sense of rectitude that comes from the repeated verticals at Grace and St. Peter's Episcopal Church, to the cheerful sunlight that shines on a corner of the portico of Hackerman House, which boasts one of the happiest histories of any building in Baltimore.

One can clearly see reflected in DuSel's work the influences of which he speaks. All of them come from the first century of photography. And not only the preponderance of his sensibility but also his techniques and materials are of that period.

He works in black and white and photographs using existing light. The large-format view camera with which he took all but two of the pictures in this book—over a period of fifteen or more years, by the way, certainly not rushing it—is the same kind of camera used by Atget and Evans.

The camera and the equipment that go with it require the contemplative approach DuSel mentions with respect to Evans. It's heavy, you don't want to move it around more than you have to, and the 8- by 10-inch sheet film it takes costs about two dollars per sheet. So it doesn't lend itself to clicking a lot of shots. It requires advance thought, which suits DuSel's temperament. "I prefer to think it out. For the most part I approach the subject one way, and I pretty much know how the picture should turn out. At Fort McHenry, for instance, it's a huge place, and a person with a 35-millimeter mindset could end up with 150 or so pictures. But I took two."

Two other aspects of using a view camera reinforce the contemplative approach. The lens throws an upside-down image on the ground glass one looks through, making the image look more abstract and compositional than descriptive. And, as DuSel has noted, isolating oneself from the peripheral scene by putting a dark cloth over one's head and the camera makes possible virtually total concentration on the image.

With extremely rare exceptions, DuSel doesn't crop the image he shoots. He thinks that's cheating—the photographer should have the vision to decide on the image when he takes the picture, and not have to do it in the darkroom. He also deplores the fact

that to crop usually prevents the viewer from having a sense of where the photographer was placed in relation to the subject, cited by Robinson as an important element of experiential photography. As an example, look at the photograph of School 33 Art Center, the one photograph in the book that DuSel cropped because he couldn't get where he wanted to be in relation to the building. As a result, one doesn't have the same sense of relationship to either the image or the building as one does elsewhere.

In the darkroom, DuSel makes prints the same size as the film sheets, 8 by 10 inches, and uses a developing formula called pyrogallol and silver chloride printing paper, both introduced in the nineteenth century. Clarity, richness of tone, visibility of detail in light and dark areas are among the attributes resulting from DuSel's processes and materials.

But equally, the overall character of his images seems totally in keeping with the subject matter. Everything from DuSel's sensibility, to his black-and-white photography, to his type of camera, to his developing formula and printing paper comes from the nineteenth and early twentieth centuries, as does the great majority of his Baltimore subjects.

And that, in turn, is in keeping with Baltimore.

Baltimore is basically a nineteenth- and early-twentieth-century city. That's when it grew from a town to one of the leading cities of the nation; when its great fortunes were made and its great philanthropists—Peabody, Pratt, Sheppard, Hopkins, Walters, etc.—bestowed; when its park, transit, school, water, and sewer systems were developed; when it expanded to its present city limits; when its major in-town suburbs, such as Roland Park and Guilford, were developed; and when it took on the architectural character which, with a few exceptions, it still retains.

Mount Vernon Place is the heart of Baltimore. It has been called "America's finest urban space" by no less a figure than the late architecture critic Lewis Mumford, in large part because it is a treasury of nineteenth- and early-twentieth-century design, in both architecture and landscaping. In terms of landscaping, the parks owe their design partly to the nineteenth-century genius Frederick Law Olmsted and partly to the early-twentieth-century landscape architect Thomas Hastings. In terms of its mostly domestic architecture, it is a catalogue of nineteenth-century styles from Classical Revival through Gothic Revival, Renaissance Revival, touches of Italianate, brownstone façades, Romanesque Revival, Chateauesque, and Beaux-Arts.

The period of Baltimore's growth and the development of its architectural character have their complement in the tremendous nineteenth-century art collections of the city. The Walters Art Museum has a great collection of nineteenth-century art, mainly French but with some American, especially that of Baltimorean Alfred Jacob Miller. The Baltimore Museum of Art has the huge, approaching 20,000-work, Lucas Collection of nineteenth-century art, mainly prints with some paintings and drawings. The Baltimore Museum of Art's world-famous Cone Collection consists principally of early-twentieth- and late-nineteenth-century works. The Maryland Historical Society and the Baltimore Museum of Art have extraordinary collections of nineteenth-century decorative arts, primarily furniture and silver.

So it is more than appropriate that this collection of photographs taken in Baltimore should reflect that nineteenth- to early-twentieth-century emphasis in three ways: the subject matter of most of the pictures, the interest of the photographer in that period of pho-tographic history, and the fact that his style and manner of working descend from that period. DuSel is not a native Baltimorean, but he has lived here for more than half his life, and his interests fit perfectly the history of his adopted city.

Art is so often approached with such deadly seriousness that people tend to forget that, aside from serving any other purpose, it exists for the enjoyment of the viewer. A group of seven DuSel photographs of partial columns reflects, among other things, Jim's sense of humor. The text accompanying that group ends, "Individually, and to a greater degree collectively, these pictures testify to the nature of art as serious fun."

As Jim cautioned, during a conversation in preparation for my writing the introduction, "The book is basically about getting people to see and think, and they don't need a lot of baggage. The shorter it is the more likely they are to read it."

There's probably too much baggage here, so it's past time to end this.

Have serious fun.

Look Again

IN BALTIMORE

Maryland Institute College of Art, main building, 1300 West Mount Royal Avenue, 1908, Pell and Corbett, architects

Of the classical-related architectural revivals at the turn of the twentieth century, this building belongs to the Renaissance Revival. Although its exterior marble cladding may be reminiscent of Venice, its mass and fenestration are based on Florentine palaces such as the Strozzi or the Medici-Riccardi. The second-floor windows, with their double arches beneath a centered bullet-hole-like opening, descend from both of those palaces and are nicely echoed by the second-floor windows at the Mount Royal Station building down the street, which the Institute also owns. The barrel-vaulted entrance leads to this central court, with an arcade on three sides and the stairway occupying the fourth.

The stairway possesses limitless possibilities of symbolism, grandeur, and drama, nowhere more effectively realized than in Italy: think of Antonio Rizzo's Scala dei Giganti at the Doge's Palace, of Bernini's exaggerated perspectives at the Vatican's Scala Regia, of the stairs that punctuate the fountained vistas at Pirro Ligurio's Villa d'Este, of the sweeping and swooping flights (stuff of an acrophobe's nightmares) in Piranesi's prison scenes. How appropriate, then, that the central hall of the Maryland Institute College of Art's Renaissance building possesses a staircase of pomp and curvature. Never mind that it's too steep, too big for its interior space, and rises to dim, anticlimactic doorways; it still has oomph.

Here, the camera's placement creates geometries to complement those it recognizes, in particular the triangle and the trapezoid. And if the angle of vision makes those stairs look daunting, more challenging still are the implications of this image: how undergraduate dreams fade and aspirations narrow as the ladder of years ascends; how promising beginnings too often peter out in lightless bureaucratic cubbyholes; how easily the loftiest intentions get corrupted by venal temptations, as alluring as the gleam of those serpentine stair rails slithering down to offer orbs of what looks like gold. But behind all the evident symbolism lies a sliver of hope in the fact that nothing here appears complete—not the staircase, not the walls, not the arch, not the doorway up there at the top—and as long as incompleteness persists, there's yet room for those limitless possibilities.

Oakland Spring House, on the grounds of the Baltimore Museum of Art, Art Museum Drive near Charles and 31st streets, ca. 1812, Benjamin H. Latrobe, architect

This building originally stood on the grounds of Robert Goodloe Harper's estate, Oakland. It resided near the present Springhouse Lane, east of Falls Road and across from Cross Keys in what is now Roland Park. Latrobe designed several buildings for Oakland, of which this Ionic-porched building, perhaps based on the Temple on the Ilissus, Athens (449 B.C.), is the only survivor and, based on what people in the early nineteenth century wrote about it, was probably the most beautiful. Generally called the spring house now, but more accurately a dairy, it was referred to in collector Robert Gilmor's 1827 diary as "the prettiest building at Oakland" (*A Guide to Baltimore Architecture*, 1997, p. 316). A letter of one Henry Gilpin said it stood "in a fine grove with a turf like emerald itself" (p. 315). So it was definitely supposed to be not just utilitarian but an architectural gem.

Benjamin Latrobe's greatest extant building, the Basilica of the Assumption, has as its Baltimore stablemate the lovely little Oakland Spring House of about 1812, originally located on an estate that became part of Roland Park but now residing on the grounds of the Baltimore Museum of Art. The massive, complex, ponderous, and imposing Basilica finds the perfect foil in Latrobe's delicate, simple, fresh little building in the form of a Greek temple, and there couldn't be a better opportunity for the comment the artist here provides on the relationship between the classical and the romantic.

Typically, the classical tends toward order, symmetry, stasis, closed or finite form, and clarity of statement, while the romantic tends toward freedom, asymmetry, movement, open or infinite form, and subtle, nuanced utterance. Generally, man makes the classical—think columns and arches—while the romantic finds its fullest expression in containment-defying nature. Here, the photo reverses all that: it cuts off the pediment, the columns, the doorway, leaving them jarringly incomplete and implying continuance beyond the seen; in particular the triangle that the viewer knows to be the pediment's

form looks maimed, while nature by contrast has been rigidly contained in two unequal but complementary and similarly proportioned right triangles. Then, too, nuance and uncertainty exist here in the shadow that flickers across the wall under the portico's ceiling, while nature appears in silhouette, all black on white, no shades of meaning there. And why has the artist engaged in this table-turning? Quite possibly to provoke rumination on the very relationship he reverses. As we are most likely to be grateful for sight in the presence of the sightless, since it doesn't otherwise come to mind, so a violation of the aesthetic norm brings that very norm to mind.

*Guilford reservoir, south of Old
Cold Spring Lane a few blocks
east of Charles Street between
Millbrook and Underwood roads*

Among America's leading architects, H. H. Richardson was the shortest-lived, the most influential, and the only one to have his name permanently attached to a style, Richardsonian Romanesque. When he died in 1886 he was only forty-seven, at the peak of his powers and of his career. Living in the period of Victorian revivals, he, too, reached back to the past, especially the Romanesque past, but in order to create an original and massively beautiful architecture that reflected his concept of the strength and spaciousness of America. His influence was prodigious, less because of his contemporary imitators, who were legion, than because his example profoundly affected the work of Louis Sullivan and Frank Lloyd Wright, who with him raised American architecture to a major position. Though some of his work is gone, fortunately much remains, from Trinity Church in Boston to the Allegheny County Courthouse and Jail in Pittsburgh, his education buildings at Harvard, and his superb houses and small libraries. All of them are as immediately and unmistakably Richardson to us as his immense presence and personality were to his contemporaries. He was also, by the way, a perceptive enthusiast and collector of architectural photography.

There are no Richardson buildings in Baltimore, though there are a couple of respectable Richardsonian efforts, the former Mercantile Safe Deposit and Trust Company building of 1886 by Wyatt and Sperry at Calvert and Redwood streets, and Baldwin and Pennington's Maryland Club of 1891 at Charles and Eager streets. And here one finds a minor reflection of the style in the heavy, rough-cut stone and rounded arch of this Guilford reservoir wall of 1893. Moreover, the composition of the photograph reinforces the likeness: one can see a kinship with Richardson's small memorial libraries, especially the one at Quincy, Massachusetts, with its off-center gabled entrance, to the left of which is a protruding stair tower, and then a low wall with a row of windows above, the last represented here by the marching fence. Thus a structure of little importance takes on stature and dignity when presented in an image that relates it to significant architecture.

THE COLUMN:
PREGNANT WITH MEANING
AND SERIOUS FUN

This page:

Rotunda, 40th Street between Roland Avenue and Keswick Road. For architectural description, see page 143.

Opposite page:

Washington Monument, Mount Vernon and Washington places, Charles and Monument streets, 1815–29, Robert Mills, architect

Mills entered the architectural competition for the design of the monument late and his monumental column was obviously the most expensive submission, but fortunately the judges of the competition picked it anyway. Fortunately as well, balconies, inscriptions, and other decorations in the original design were later discarded by Mills, for the simple column we have is stronger and more handsome than the original design. Rising to a total height of 178 feet, the monument has a square base with a museum room surrounding the bottom of the column, which rises from the base to be crowned by a statue of Washington, resigning his commission at Annapolis in 1883, by Italian sculptor Enrico Causici. The monument is open some days a week, and people can climb 228 steps to windows in the base of the statue with fine views.

From the Acropolis in Athens to the Roman Forum to the façades of official Washington, the column in architecture is as ubiquitous and pregnant with meaning as the tree in nature. It can stand for ambition, strength, rectitude, power, sexuality, and in its ruined state for the destruction of all of that, the ultimate failure of human strivings. With its symbolic and rhythmic potential and its capacity for chiaroscuro effects, the column has been a constant favorite with photographers, from Louis de Clerq's partly buried colonnade at Edfu (1859) and Edouard Baldus's marching pairs in the cloister at St. Trophime (ca. 1861) to Frederick Evans's column clusters at Bourges (1900) and Ezra Stoller's single soarer at Dulles Airport (1964).

This group of photographs focuses on parts of still whole and functioning columns, not ruins, as examples of the column's nature and the photographer's ways of using it. The two column bases from the Rotunda on 40th Street reveal the paradox of the column's immense strength and how its mass can be dissolved by light. The shaft of the Washington Monument against the sky shows the reverse, how form can be defined by light and dissolved by shadow, as the column's roundness appears to flatten out and come to an edge as thin and sharp as that of a piece of paper. The two solid, truncated columns at World Relief Headquarters at Baltimore and Charles streets are enfolded by a play of flowing shadow, hinting at the attraction of sexual opposites. The

Opposite page:
World Relief Headquarters,
Baltimore and Charles streets,
1907, Palmer and Thomas,
architects

Inspired by the Erectheum on the Acropolis in Athens, the former Savings Bank of Baltimore's entrance front on Baltimore Street has a portico with four massive columns supporting a pediment, and there are six equally impressive columns along the Charles Street side. The column bases' ornaments and the lions' heads on the cornice were made from casts that came from Athens. The interior, originally one immense banking room, was turned into two floors in the 1950s.

This page:
Metal street pole with signs
attached, Keswick Road between
40th Street and University
Parkway

Above:
*Porch columns, Roland Park
between Roland Avenue and
Falls Road*

Opposite page:
*Scottish Rite Temple of Free-
masonry, Charles and 39th
streets. For architectural description, see page 52.*

vertical metal cylinder that lifts a street light and does double duty holding up two traffic signs shows the column form as anonymous urban worker, and the juxtaposition of these surfaces with the foliage behind them contrasts man-made solidity with natural grace. The Roland Park porch columns in front of a tree blurred by the breeze curiously leave a double impression: art is long, life is short and transient; but life is at least free to move, to change, to feel. The column shafts rising from their bases at the top of a flight of stairs at the Scottish Rite Temple of Freema-sonry at Charles and 39th streets sug-gest human aspiration more effectively than if they were shown whole, and the picture's complex layering of space and solid form allows the eye to play tricks upon itself, turning void into mass and volume into plane. The trio of columns shown in stark white against the gray walls of the porch, also at the Scottish Rite Temple, sets up another trompe l'oeil effect, in which the walls come forward to read as fragments of an image on a blank white background.

Individually, and to a greater degree collectively, these pictures testify to the nature of art as serious fun.

Whole Foods, 1340 Smith Avenue, Mount Washington, ca. 1900, architect unknown

Originally part of the Port Washington Cotton Company's complex, the building subsequently became part of the Maryland Bolt & Nut Company. In 1936, a fire burned out the interior wood timber supports, and the following year it was built back with steel beams. Since 1989, the complex has been owned by Washingtonville Limited Partnership. The owners put the building in usable shape, essentially respecting its form (e.g., replacing the clerestory windows with a new set), Werner Mueller, architect.

In architecture as in nature the fittest survive, and for the last two thousand years or so the basilica form has been a notable survivor. The word *basilica* originally derived from Greek words meaning king and royal, but in Rome a basilica was a building, variously used as a place for tribunals to sit, for public assemblies, or for a market.

The form of the basilica was simple and specific. It had a taller central aisle or nave, flanked by lower side aisles separated from the nave by rows of columns. At one end the building extended outward in a semicircular form known as an apse. The early Christians appropriated the basilica form for their churches, and thus it has come down to us. The clerestory (or more understandably the clearstory), or row of windows down either side of the nave walls above the roofs of the side aisles, is a feature most commonly associated with Gothic churches, but it actually goes all the way back to ancient Egyptian architecture.

All of the major elements of the basilica form are either present or implied in this former industrial building, standing empty several years ago when this image captured its austere beauty and understated rectitude. Imagine

the steel posts as stone pillars, imagine the windows filled with stained glass, imagine the double tier of windows at the far end bowed into semicircular shape, and you have your cathedral. And what could be more fitting than a church form here, for when this building was new, about a century ago, industry was America's national religion as well as its engine. If it is no longer such, in our service- and technology-oriented age, it has nevertheless left us some handsome relics such as this.

Once they have lost their original function, those buildings fittest to survive are the ones for which an adaptive reuse can be found. This one filled the bill and has become Whole Foods supermarket in Mount Washington, historically appropriate since a market was one of the functions a Roman basilica served. But one can no longer see the building's interior form as clearly as in this photograph. Thank goodness for the photograph—one can say that this work of architecture's Boswell found it.

Built for Ernest Jenkins, a member of the family that owned extensive property in the area, the house has been owned by Boys' Latin School since 1970. Called Georgian in a school publication, its four-column portico with the tripartite window above (though without the Palladian central arch) resembles the main façade of Mount Clare (p. 163) from the 1760s, while the third-floor central lunette recalls that on Mount Clare's garden façade, added in 1787 in the then-ascendant Federal style. True to Fowler, the building is handsomely proportioned and detailed; for example, as shown here, he created third-floor dormers that appear crisp, neat, and compact both outside and inside.

Strange as it may seem, this picture is about love.

A dormer is a vertical architectural element, containing a window, which projects out from a pitched roof; but here, thanks to the photographer having captured the dynamic contrast between light and shadow, the dormer plays the active role of a visitor entering the room. In its sharp-angled whiteness, the top of this form resembles the crisply starched cap of a nun, announcing the presence of its wearer, who brings the light of hope and life into the rooms of those who suffer.

At the very end of Thornton Wilder's diminutive great novel *The Bridge of San Luis Rey,* written in a style so pure it approaches the sublime, such a scene takes place. An abbess of a convent visits a room of the sick at night, her lantern at her side, to speak words of comfort to the patients. There is a visitor to the convent that night, the daughter of one of five people killed when the famous bridge of San Luis Rey fell some time earlier. The abbess, as she speaks with the visitor at her side, thinks of the accident and its victims.

"But even while she was talking, other thoughts were passing in the back of her mind. 'Even now,' she thought, 'almost no one remembers Esteban and Pepita, but myself. Camila alone remembers her uncle Pio and her son; this woman, her mother. But soon we shall die and all memory of those five will have left the earth, and we ourselves shall be loved for a while and forgotten. But the love will have been enough; all those impulses of love return to the love that made them. Even memory is not necessary for love. There is a land of the living and a land of the dead and the bridge is love, the only survival, the only meaning'" (1969, pp. 179–80).

Prince Hall Masons Masonic Temple, former Temple Oheb Shalom, Eutaw Place and Lanvale Street, 1893, Joseph E. Sperry, architect

The triple-domed building of Beaver Dam marble, in what has been called overall a Byzantine style, has other references, not seen here, to Renaissance Revival—the side windows compare with those on the Maryland Institute College of Art building and the Mount Royal Station building. But especially when seen as a whole the building holds together. The interior is considerably lighter in feeling than the exterior, a single room with half-domes, arches and vaults, and woodwork of quartered oak. Sperry, long a noted Baltimore architect, is best known for this building, the old Mercantile Safe Deposit and Trust Company building at Calvert and Redwood streets, and the Bromo-Seltzer Tower at Eutaw and Lombard streets.

Now the Prince Hall Masons Masonic Temple, this building at Eutaw Place and Lanvale Street on the edge of Bolton Hill debuted in 1893 as the Temple Oheb Shalom and was long known as the Eutaw Place Temple. The architect was Joseph Evans Sperry, one of the best of his time in Baltimore. A guidebook to Baltimore architecture calls the design Byzantine. While the building looks more or less of a piece when seen from a distance, this delicious detail of it shows that the term *Byzantine* may be less relevant in the architectural sense than the adjectival sense, if by Byzantine one means complicated, confusing, and even deliberately obscure.

For Sperry drew from a grab-bag of stylistic bits and pieces. The domes, with their tile roofs, minimal indentations, and little outward flips at the bottom, are slightly onionated, a more or less Byzantine characteristic but handled here with timidity. There is nothing at all Byzantine about a cupola crowning a dome, a Renaissance or Georgian touch, this one looking as if it might have come off of an English eighteenth-century country house such as Houghton Hall in Norfolk. The rough-cut white stone walls and row of narrow arches owe something

to Richardsonian Romanesque, but the column capitals under the arches are classically influenced and so delicate as to be almost Adamesque. The balustrade or gallery atop this loggia-like element, and the round windows under the dome above, have a Renaissance flavor. Classical pilasters separate the windows under the main dome, each of which includes a Star of David surrounded by what looks like a Roman laurel wreath. Finally, the walls below the main dome are clad in shingles that look like they might have been left over from a house in Roland Park.

An eclectic mixture to say the least, a hodgepodge, a mishmash, but it all adds up to a curiously integrated whole, to Sperry's credit. He knew what he was doing.

Two of the eighty-one images in photographer Alfred Stieglitz's portrait of Georgia O'Keeffe show one of her hands and a bit of arm posed against the gleaming black-and-chrome spare tire case of her Ford V-8. There's no hand here, but compositionally and tonally and in other ways as well this photograph of the flat end and round mouth of a cannon bears a striking resemblance to one of those two Stieglitz photos.

Here the small circular mouth of the cannon appears at the upper left, while part of another circle, the rim of the cannon's front end, enters at the upper right and exits at the lower left. The Stieglitz photograph has much the reverse, with the chrome hubcap at lower left and the chrome rim of the tire case entering at upper left and exiting at lower right. In both cases there is a very shallow depth of field, and in both cases there's a progression of contrasts between light and dark from "front" to "back." In the Stieglitz the progression is light, dark, light, darker, darkest, while in the image opposite it's dark, light, dark, lighter, lightest.

Both pictures also offer thematic contrasts. In the Stieglitz there is the contrast of the hand, organic and rather awkwardly posed with splayed fingers, but tonally warm and suggesting both human warmth and human uniqueness, shown against the cold, gleaming, mass-produced, geometric perfection of the tire case. In the photograph opposite, there's the contrast of the artist having made an agreeable aesthetic object out of an instrument of death.

Finally, in both cases one sees an object that most of us would pay little attention to elevated to a higher plane through the artist's vision, a testament to the fact that when one has a true vision any means can be used to express it and show the artist's mind at work. There's as much of Stieglitz as of O'Keeffe in his multiple portraits, and the photographs herein are as much about the photographer as about architecture, or Baltimore, or photography. That's what O'Keeffe meant when she said of Stieglitz, "His eye was in him, and he used it on anything that was near by. Maybe that way he was always photographing himself" (*Georgia O'Keeffe: A Portrait by Alfred Stieglitz*, 1997, introduction).

*Mount Vernon Place United
Methodist Church, Mount
Vernon and Washington places,
Charles and Monument streets,
1872, Dixon and Carson,
architects*

The main exterior features of
the building are its three towers, the caliper-like relieving
arch around the rose window,
and the polychrome appearance, primarily gray-green sandstone from Baltimore County
and brown sandstone trim.
The interior contains cast-iron
columns supporting balconies
and a series of wooden arches
and trusses with wrought-iron
scrollwork. The west side has a
row of clerestory windows.

Of all the revivals of the Victorian era,
the Gothic was by far the most popular in architecture, and this picture of
a corner of the Mount Vernon Place
United Methodist Church has something to say about why. Aside from the
religious impetus and a more general-
ized longing for the past, the Gothic
Revival perfectly satisfied and perhaps
helped create the Victorian passion
for stuff and clutter. It was the age of
gewgaw and gimcrack, of knickknack
and bric-a-brac; every surface had to be
embellished, and every embellishment,
of speech as well as visual ornamentation, was thought to be improved by
repetition. In this snippet of the church
building twenty pointed arches can
be found, and countless leaf and petal
motifs, along with a couple of charm-
ing surprises—have you spotted the
bird and the ears of corn? In addition
to all of its sculptural embellishments,
its traceried rose window, and its two
towers with their dozens of little tur-
rets and arches, the church front's flat
surfaces are faced with a combination
of brown and green stone, all of which
adds up to the busiest façade in Baltimore.

An 1888 guide to the city declared,
"No picture, unless carefully colored,
and no mere description can give the
reader a notion of its appearance" (*A
Guidebook to Baltimore Architecture*,
1997, p. 126). This photo gives the lie to
that, proving that often a detail can be
more revealing than an overall view. In
addition to the multiplicity of decorative
motifs, it shows the variety of surfaces,
textures, and tones far better than any
replication of the entire façade would
do. Perhaps even better than a visit to
the church—presented with the whole
thing, one usually sees little if any detail—this photograph gives us a sense
of the nature of the building as a work
of architecture. While a lot offers itself
for notice here, none of it possesses any
unusual aesthetic merit, and despite
its status as a beloved landmark much
the same can be said of the church as a
whole. It is Baltimore's most thorough
example of architectural Babbittry:
respectable but not grand and soaring,
provincial and damn proud of it.

*School 33 Art Center, 1427 Light
Street, 1890, designer unknown*

According to Peter Kurtze of the
Maryland Historical Trust, who
has studied Baltimore school
buildings, between about
1870 and 1895 the city, to save
money, had many public buildings designed by one or another
person in the office of the
building inspector of the city
of Baltimore. When an outside
architect was hired, the name
is given when discussing the
building in the annual reports
of the building inspector's
office. When no name is given,
that indicates that a member of
the building inspector's office
staff designed the building. No
name is given in the records
of 1889, 1890, or 1891 for an
architect of School 33 or for
the identical building, known
as School 32, at the corner of
Lanvale Street and Guilford
Avenue.

Sometimes a building of no great distinction as a whole nevertheless has
elements worth noticing. The former
Baltimore public school number 33, on
Light Street in South Baltimore, is one
of the city's most successful examples
of adaptive reuse of architecture. Since
1979 it has been School 33 Art Center,
a nonprofit institution that mounts
consistently interesting exhibitions of
contemporary regional art, leases stu-
dios to worthy artists at modest rents,
and has art courses for children and
adults.

The two-story building, opened
in 1890, has a modest Richardsonian
Romanesque look, by a designer whose
name is unknown. On the whole it
is not notable architecture, but it has
some reasonably pleasing details.

The curved brickwork around the
windows and on both the free-standing
and attached columns gives those elements a look of refinement. (The awkward brickwork where the two window
arches meet occurs on the identical
building at Lanvale Street and Guilford
Avenue.) The lack of indentation or any
sort of visual break in the brickwork
where the attached capital joins the
building has the effect of making the

surface here feel like skin drawn taut
over an inner body. It's thus reminiscent of the surfaces of H. H. Richardson's shingle-style houses, especially
the Stoughton House in Cambridge,
Massachusetts, just eight years older
than this building.

The brownstone trim is the building's best feature. The courses running across the façade underneath the
windows and at the bottoms of their
arches are nicely proportioned in relation to one another (about two to one),
are rough-cut in good Richardsonian
fashion, and provide a satisfying contrast in texture to the smooth brick
surfaces. The smooth-cut cornice
defining the angle of the porch's roof,
and the triangle of decorative brickwork
beneath it, present a strong diagonal
that complements both the horizontality of the brick and stone courses and
the verticality of the narrow windows.
The column capitals provide the finest decorative touch of all; the upper
surfaces have a stippled appearance
somewhat akin to repousse silver, and
at the corners are ram's-horn spirals
based on Ionic capitals. Such a classical
touch on a Romanesque building may
be thought wrong, but it has its prece-

dents in the original Romanesque period (e.g., at Saint Aignan-sur-Cher in France) and also in Richardson buildings including the Allegheny County Courthouse in Pittsburgh of 1883–88. Besides, the capitals are handsome and look quite appropriate.

A personal confession may help to point out that the part can serve better than the whole. I have done work on three editions of a book on Baltimore architecture over a period of more than thirty years, from the 1960s to the 1990s. And in fourteen years as art critic of the Baltimore Sun I paid more than a hundred visits to School 33. I was aware of the building's style and materials, but I never noticed those column capitals until I saw this photograph.

Greek Orthodox Cathedral of the Annunciation, Maryland Avenue and Preston Street, 1889, Charles E. Cassell, architect

This Romanesque Revival building with Byzantine influence was constructed as a Presbyterian church and continued as one until 1934; it has housed a Greek Orthodox congregation since 1937. The building is of Port Deposit granite with polished marble columns, carved stone decoration, and four pairs of oak entrance doors, two curved. The interior consists of a semicircular auditorium with Tiffany stained-glass windows, a 1960s flat ceiling under the original trusses supporting the roof, and a balcony extended and made curvilinear in the 1980s.

Placement of the camera here resulted in an image that reveals what this building might have been, but isn't. It shows what the architect wanted to do, but didn't quite know how to do.

The architect, Charles E. Cassell (ca. 1838–1916), was a designer of competence rather than genius. He was prolific and popular, and had a certain status in his time, attested to by the fact that he was selected to design two buildings on Mount Vernon Place and Washington Place in the 1890s, when that quartet of squares was in its prime as the home of the social elite. Unfortunately, they were and remain the two aesthetically worst buildings there, the Stafford Hotel and the Severn Apartments, both too tall for the domestic scale of the Places and also not attractive. Cassell's best surviving jobs are the Greenway Cottages on 40th Street (1874), now part of Roland Park Place, and this church building at Maryland Avenue and Preston Street, erected in 1889 for the Associated Reform Church and since the 1930s a Greek Orthodox church, now cathedral.

Cassell designed it in the Richardsonian Romanesque style just then beginning to wane in fashion—meaning, among other things, that it had recently

arrived in Baltimore. The building has an odd but interesting feature, its completely rounded front end, but it also has a fatal flaw. An essential ingredient of the best Richardsonian Romanesque is asymmetry, and here the symmetry of the façade when seen in person leaves an impression of the precious and effete. It was precisely the idea of the finished—the complete and therefore exhausted—European civilization that Richardson sought to counter with a style that would reflect, on the contrary, the youth and vitality of America. Cassell for some reason didn't understand that.

This photograph does. Its asymmetry reinforces the strength of the building's rough-cut stone, low rounded arches, and horizontality. It also leaves a sense of the unfinished, of becoming rather than being, and therefore of youthful energy, which symmetry can never do. And by bringing the viewer up close to the marching columns and arches and the overall heaviness offset by lighter decorative touches, it brings out the building's virtues better than a view of the whole can do. In short, the photographer creates the essence the building was supposed to possess, and thus shows a better sense of what Cassell was trying for than Cassell had.

At first glance there appears no doubt about which is the more baroque of this duet of arch-clustered spaces, or which the more rewarding photograph. Any Baltimorean asked to name the city's finest interior spaces would surely include the central courtyard of the Walters Art Museum, designed in 1905 by New York architect and Walters in-law William Delano and based on the 1630s Palazzo dell'Universita by Genoa's best baroque architect, Bartolomeo Bianchi. In Baltimore as in Genoa, arches supported by double columns frame the space, and here the strong light pumps up the dramatic possibilities by producing lengthy shadows which also, together with the diagonal view, create an illusion of deeper space than exists—all in good baroque tradition.

By contrast, the other photograph, of the substructure of the Kelly Avenue bridge in Mount Washington, can seem prosaic and boring. Instead of pristine marble, moisture-stained concrete. Instead of a gleaming polished floor, pebble-strewn dirt. The arches' supports, hardly worthy of the name *columns,* descend to clunky square bases or none at all, and the gray light shambles along, creating half-hearted shadows that peter out in whimpers and sighs.

If that's what your lying eyes tell you, look again. Only peer through the layer of artifice in the Walters picture and it's easy to recognize the space's self-contained regularity, benign and psychologically comfortable. Standing where the photographer has placed us in the other picture, however, we have no idea where we are in relation to the structure, how big it is, what shape it has, where it starts and stops. It's as uncompassable as tomorrow, and therefore both intriguing and ominous. Space leaks out, we have no control over it, so we experience a visual image as open, flowing, and dynamic as the constantly rolling present, with a finitude as unknowable as the moment of death.

And there's a great deal more here: an essay in grays, another in textures, areas of wall surface with drips and splotches reminiscent of passages from abstract expressionist art of the 1950s, and an invitation to consider whether what's pictured has architectural interest. Initially there would seem to be no doubt about that, either. It was designed (if indeed it was designed at all) by an engineer, not an architect. It lacks a style, it has no façades, it was not intended to make an aesthetic statement. All true, and all equally true of the Pont du Gard.

Next spread, left:
Walters Art Museum, South Washington Place, 600 North Charles Street, 1905–9, Delano and Aldrich, architects

The original building of the Walters Art Museum is Renaissance in feel. The exterior, with a rusticated first floor below a wall with pilasters and blind windows surmounted by a frieze, is descended from the mid-nineteenth-century Hotel Pourtales in Paris, which was in turn based on architect Felix Duban's knowledge of the architecture of Renaissance Florence, as stated in William R. Johnston's book *William and Henry Walters, the Reticent Collectors* (1999, p. 68). The interior contains a series of galleries on two floors around a two-story courtyard based on the Palazzo dell'Universita or Palazzo Balbi of seventeenth-century Genoa, with a double staircase and arcades on both floors. (See also p. 108 for the Walters's 1974 building and p. 56 for Hackerman House, the Walters's Asian art museum.)

Next spread, right:
Kelly Avenue bridge, Falls Road and Kelly Avenue, Mount Washington

Green Mount Cemetery Chapel,
1501 Greenmount Avenue, 1856,
Niernsee and Neilson, architects

The Gothic Revival chapel, sited on a rise in the cemetery, is visible for blocks around. The exterior has a 102-foot spire, flying buttresses, pinnacles and tracery in the English Gothic style, and an octagonal shape with porte-cochere, all faced in brownstone. One of the interior's features is a stained-glass dome placed under the tower.

In his fine novel *The Reader,* German author Bernhard Schlink has his protagonist pose questions without answers. The novel is told in the first person by a man who, when a teenager in the 1960s, had a love affair with an older woman who later goes on trial for having participated in an atrocity when she was a Nazi concentration camp guard. The situation brings to the narrator's mind questions whose implications reach far beyond the Holocaust and Germany to touch on the nature and utility of guilt.

"What should our second generation have done, what should it do with the knowledge of the horrors of the extermination of the Jews? ... Should we only fall silent in revulsion, shame and guilt? To what purpose? ... That some few would be convicted and punished while we of the second generation were silenced by revulsion, shame and guilt—was that all there was to it now?" (1997, p. 104).

To what purpose is the sense of guilt, and if to none, should one will oneself not to have it if one does, and is that possible? If guilt is to some purpose, if the feeling of guilt both individually and collectively can help to prevent the repetition of evil, should one will oneself to have it if one does not, and is that possible?

Does every German generation have an obligation to feel guilt for the Holocaust, in the hope of preventing a repetition of it? Does every human generation have the same obligation? And what does all of that have to do with this picture of the chapel at Green Mount Cemetery?

Any image of light flooding a religious interior must bring to mind photographs of religious architecture by Frederick Evans a century ago. In the book *Architecture Transformed,* photographer and art historian Cervin Robinson writes that, in Evans's photographs, light "becomes part of the experience of the subject and not, as in the earlier style, a means for showing objects with clarity" (1987, p. 78). In this photograph both light and dark become parts of the experience, and also the meaning, of an image loaded with symbolism.

The picture's structure resonates with the triple hierarchical trios of heaven, earth, and hell; God, man, and the devil; white, gray, and black. The middle by implication combines the other two, suggesting the human potential for evil and the possible neces-

sity of guilt to forestall the unleashing of that potential.

By choosing an ecclesiastical image in which the floor opens up to reveal what appears to be a dark chamber below, DuSel inevitably brings to mind dungeons and torture chambers, or in other words the Inquisition. Ah so—if Germans must forever bear guilt for the Holocaust, what about Christians and the Inquisition?

There's another level. Why are light and white always associated with God and good, black and dark with evil and the devil? "For I have sworn thee fair, and thought thee bright, / Who art as black as hell, as dark as night" (Sonnet 147). Black magic, black devil, black dog, black thoughts—what racial overtones exist in all such language expressing the negative qualities associated with black? To what extent is racism, an evil, perpetuated by the continued use of such images, both verbal and visual—in Christian churches, for example, the draping of the cross with black during Lent and the wearing of white at Easter? To what extent is the evil of those who employ such imagery not potential or retrospective but active and present?

Which leads to another question: Does the idea of retrospective guilt for the evils of older generations perhaps serve the present generation as a means of ignoring the guilt it should feel for its own evils? Questions without answers.

Sometimes a picture speaks of several things at once, as this one does. It's certainly in part about formal aspects of the photograph, especially light and composition. The light here meets some of the Basilica of the Assumption's surfaces in a way that makes them appear to radiate a light stronger than that of the sky behind, to give back the light to the day that gives it to them. Then, too, there are fine sets of echoing diagonals, especially roof ribbing and shadows.

The ladder suggests a story in itself, of the building of the structure, the alterations to it over time, and the continued maintenance of it, which together have gone on for two hundred years since Benjamin Henry Latrobe designed it in 1805 as the first Roman Catholic cathedral in the United States. Down the generations, a tale of countless human hands building to the glory of God, and not incidentally to the glory of architecture. For this is unquestionably and without close competition Baltimore's greatest work of architecture, and the surviving masterpiece of English-born Latrobe, one of the foremost architects ever to work in America. No less a figure than the eminent British architectural historian Nikolaus Pevsner called the Basilica "North America's most beautiful church."

There is the dome as dome, also Baltimore's finest and an example of what has stood the test of time, since the Romans developed it (at least in the West) as the ultimate form of architectural grandeur in many lands: the domes of the Pantheon and of St. Peter's in Rome, the dome of St. Paul's in London, the dome of the Capitol in Washington, the dome of Hagia Sophia in Istanbul, the Dome of the Rock in Jerusalem, the triple-domed Pearl Mosque and the Taj Mahal, both at Agra in India, and on and on.

If the Basilica's dome is Baltimore's finest, it has a good deal of company: the tiny dome atop the tower of St. Vincent de Paul Church near the Shot Tower; the dome of First Unitarian Church just around the corner from the Basilica; the triple domes of the former Temple Oheb Shalom, now the Prince Hall Masons Masonic Temple at Eutaw Place and Lanvale Street; the triple domes of the Berea Temple of Seventh-Day Adventists at Madison Avenue and Robert Street; the obsessively hemispherical dome of Shaarei Tfiloh Con-

36

Basilica of the Assumption, Cathedral Street between Franklin and Mulberry streets, 1805–21, Benjamin H. Latrobe, architect; later additions and alterations

In 1805, Latrobe presented two designs, one Gothic and one neoclassical, to Bishop John Carroll for the first Roman Catholic cathedral in the United States. The neoclassical design was selected, and building went on slowly long after Latrobe's death in 1821 until the complex was finally completed about 1890. In the 1940s there were alterations, including the addition of stained-glass windows, which made the interior much darker. The building is now being restored, including removal of the stained-glass windows and reopening of windows in the dome, which should make a major difference.

Despite changes, the building is undeniably Latrobe's, and his greatest extant work. The massive granite exterior walls are relieved by windows set in recessed arched panels, and

parts of the building project or recede "so that one is conscious of a well-proportioned group of geometric shapes that are carefully interrelated," wrote architectural historian Henry-Russell Hitchcock (*A Guide to Baltimore Architecture*, 1997, p. 103). The main dome sits on an octagonal drum, and its "rotund gravity," according to architectural historian Charles Brownell (p. 102), is complemented by the lightness of the onion domes of the two front towers. The interior has received and deserves the highest praise. The central dome dominates the space and is echoed by saucer domes to the east and west. The rotunda's width encompasses both nave and side aisles, so that all spaces lead to and out of the center, giving a sense of fluid movement and unity. The integration of all the parts and the perfect balance of mass and space contribute to the interior's extraordinary beauty.

gregation at Auchentoroly Terrace and Liberty Heights Avenue; the dome on the original building of Johns Hopkins Hospital on Broadway, and so on.

Back in 1968 John Dos Passos, in a delightful essay on Baltimore's architecture, wrote, "A few years ago I drove a sharp-eyed friend around who could not ever remember having looked at the town carefully before. 'Why it's a city of domes,' he cried out, 'a city of domes and spires'" (*A Guide to Baltimore Architecture*, 1997, p. xvi).

The mass of Baltimoreans, if they ever thought of their city that way, haven't been inclined to do so since tall buildings generally overwhelmed the domes and spires and took away their status as landmarks. But back about 1830 the artist W. H. Bartlett, in his series of American city views, created one of Baltimore that made it look so beautifully sited on the water and so dominated by the dome of the then-new cathedral rising above the town that the print has come to be known as the "Constantinople view" of Baltimore. Latrobe, who by then was dead, would have been pleased.

The building of Roland Park in the early twentieth century coincided with a style in architecture and decorative arts known as Arts and Crafts, based on a combination of influences including the Jugendstil and the Wiener Werkstatte in Vienna, William Morris in England, and Charles Rennie Mackintosh in Scotland. The style featured forthright design, solid craftsmanship, and angular—often rectangular—rather than curving design motifs. It has made something of a comeback with the recent rise in popularity and prices of the furniture of Gustav Stickley. A few decades ago you could hardly give the stuff away, but now the major pieces sell for up to hundreds of thousands of dollars.

In Arts and Crafts design, as with every other style after the early nineteenth century, Baltimore was not a leader of fashion, either chronologically or aesthetically. But about 1911 Edward L. Palmer, later to become better known as half of the architecture firm of Palmer and Lamdin, designed a group of mostly handsome Arts and Crafts–influenced houses around a small triangular interior park in northern Roland Park. Near that triangle, facing Falls Road and putting a period to the western end of Edgevale Road, stands this little stucco-clad structure, probably also designed by Palmer, which in its shapes, proportions, and decorative touches has a definite Arts and Crafts feel to it. Nicely, it's still put to the use for which it was designed, to provide shelter for people awaiting transit vehicles, back then streetcars and now buses.

Today it also provides a clean slate for the graffitist, to either decorate or deface, depending on your point of view. Sometime after this picture was taken in 1999, the walls received a partial coat of blue paint to cover the graffiti seen here, but a new generation has appeared, either by the same graffitist or one who employs a quite similar style of expression.

It's appealing that this humble little structure was given a touch of style originally, and that it has survived essentially unchanged for almost a century. And it's also appealing that the photographer noticed it. If I sound especially sentimental about it, I live just a block away, across the street from the Palmer triangle. When this book appears, people in various parts of Baltimore will come upon such unpretentious bits of their neighborhoods and enjoy a warm sense of recognition.

The Chimes, 1801 Thornbury Road, Mount Washington, built as the Mount Washington Presbyterian Church, 1878, Dixon and Carson, architects

The buttresses, battens, and braces contribute to the exterior's stick Gothic feel. The nave is a small space with dark wood trusses, altar, and pews removed so there is not as much religious flavor. The right-angled attachment to the main church building is a later addition. Chimes, Inc., now uses the building as a school for their program for children with special needs.

Formerly the Mount Washington Presbyterian Church and now The Chimes, a school for children with special needs, this ungainly building possesses manifold awkwardnesses (not all visible here), but they add up to a work of integrity if not exactly of charm. The clumsy massing, the ugly dormers that look as if they were thrown at the building with no attempt at graceful transitions, the strange-looking side entrance that seems to have been an afterthought, rooflines that meet at haphazard angles, and other gaucheries are perhaps all typical of the style known as stick Gothic. But even if so, they make the structure look as if it were designed by a committee of blind men not in communication with one another, rather than a firm of competent architects, which Dixon and Carson presumably were supposed to be when they brought this forth in 1873. With the exception of the tower, by far the best feature, it all reminds you of a pile of football players who have just dived at a fumbled ball from all directions.

But it's fun—fun to look at, fun to write about, fun to have around. It has personality, which rescues many a gawky individual from the oblivion of social neglect, and which puts it a step ahead of all the correct but dull architecture one sees everywhere. And more than a little of that personality comes from the presence—all around the building, not just in this corner—of what must be the silliest-looking flying buttresses in the history of architecture. Had you known, O builders of Notre Dame and Bourges, that the descendants of your graceful leapers might one day come to this, would you have thought again?

Baltimore Museum of Art, 10 Art Museum Drive near Charles and 31st streets. For architectural description, see page 146.

Nothing appears to move in this photograph of bare vine tendrils spread across, around, and over a massive stone wall at the Baltimore Museum of Art, but the picture nevertheless gives the viewer a sense of two kinds of movement. There's violent, rushing movement as of white water cascading down a rock-filled riverbed. And there's the movement of shadows across the afternoon lawn, so gradual as to be imperceptible from moment to moment but as ineluctable as the death of daylight they portend. The violent and rushing may be thrilling or horrible, but it is the slow and continuous that has the deeper meaning, and we all know what it is. Get thee to my lady's chamber and tell her let her paint an inch thick, to this favor she must come.

Memory, *mourning sculpture,*
by Hans Schuler, 1907, in Riggs
burial plot at Green Mount Cem-
etery, 1501 Greenmount Avenue

A generation ago, this tour de force of bronze sculpture, a figure of mourning on a graveyard monument, would have been at best dismissed as a superficial work of art and would more probably have been an object of scorn and ridicule. The show-off virtuosity of the sculptor, the overt sentimentality of the figure, its implied religiosity, its obvious costliness, and the whole idea of conspicuous grief were as out of fashion forty years or so ago as cigarettes are today.

The appearance of this photograph is a powerful reminder of the major changes recent decades have seen in attitudes of many kinds. In art, the Hellenistic and the baroque periods have returned to favor, both of them more elaborate in craftsmanship and emotional expression than their predecessors. We are today more inclined to appreciate the sculptor's ability to execute a work of such technical display, with its complicated pose, its illusion of drapery flowing over flesh, and its rose in one hand and floral wreath in the other finished down to the tiniest detail. In the mid-twentieth century, abstraction and style ruled art. Today, the representational image is back in favor, the more loaded with content and symbolism—Meaning—the better.

Changes in art always reflect changes in the culture art mirrors. The decline of the influence of the WASP aristocracy and the simultaneous decline of the idea of masculine superiority, together with the rise of religious fundamentalism and of multicultural values, have all dealt blows to the notion of emotional reserve as good form. When even Episcopalian funerals feature friends and relations of the deceased unashamedly breaking down as they address the assembled to express their love and loss, and when it is no longer a surprise to see in the newspaper pictures of burly policemen weeping in each other's arms at the memorial service for a fallen comrade, nothing could be more timely than to bring this figure to our attention.

St. John's Episcopal Church, Huntingdon, 3001 Old York Road, 1847, Robert Cary Long Jr., architect; 1859, John W. Priest, architect; 1877, Henry M. Congdon, architect

In 1858 the Long church, no picture of which survives, was the victim of arson. A year later Priest of New York, who at the time was also working on St. Luke's Church in West Baltimore, was hired to design a replacement, it is thought using the remains of the original foundation and walls. The 1859 church consisted of the present tower and nave of four bays. The transepts and chancel were added in 1877 by Congdon, successor to Priest. The present interior decorations, to a degree based on earlier work, have been done since 1980. The rectory, also built of stone and of Gothic design in keeping with the church, was built in 1868.

In the 1840s, the Ecclesiological movement in England sought to influence church architecture outside of England. Bishop William Whittingham of Maryland was a member of the Ecclesiological Society, and according to a publication of St. John's Church, Huntingdon, "through his influence St. John's was built in the Gothic style recommended for American country churches" (*A Guide to Baltimore Architecture*, 1997, p. 313).

Country is the operative word here, for while St. John's is very much in the city, just off of Greenmount Avenue at 30th Street in Waverly, it has a country feel to it. Its modest size, its setting with lawns and trees, its adjacent graveyard, and its rectory also built in the Gothic style and of rough-surfaced stone, all add up to the feel of a rural or at most a small-town church, a feel the Ecclesiological movement advocated in church design.

The church has a complicated building history, involving three architects and taking place over a period of thirty years. But happily it looks all of a piece.

This photograph of the side of the church, with the south porch in the foreground, the south transept beyond, and a bit of the graveyard at the far right, captures the rural feel of the church far better than a picture of the front would do. The tower on the front, not seen here, does not make the church look large but makes it look imposing and rather more formal than this intimate view. Moreover, the photograph has the flavor of early photography through various devices—the original printed in brown (which always produces a sense of age) and the upper roofline and tips of the tree branches dissolving into the all-white sky. One might be looking at an 1840s photograph by William Henry Fox Talbot or Edouard Baldus (the latter's Chapel of Sainte-Croix, Montmajour, thought to be from 1849, comes to mind).

Because it looks like a period photograph of a country church, this picture captures the feeling that the Ecclesiological movement sought to promote. It is probably more true to the spirit in which the church was created than any other picture ever taken of St. John's. And indeed it is more true to that spirit than St. John's looks in person.

900 block South Charles Street

The precisionists would have loved this picture. They were a group of American artists of the first half of the twentieth century, including Charles Sheeler, Charles Demuth, and Ralston Crawford, who went the other way from the then-dominant American regionalists. As the latter pictured rural America, the precisionists limned industrial and urban America, concentrating on clean lines and the geometries of often reduced forms. Their art was a forerunner of geometric abstraction and minimalism, but in the hands of Sheeler it often included a level of emotion, such as high drama in his *Church Street El* (1920), or intense loneliness in his *Manchester* (1949) at the Baltimore Museum of Art. Precisionism's planar, even analytical images owed something to cubism, but they turned away from that art's intimacy and preciosity, and instead championed American bigness and muscularity.

Here we have all of that: urban America, industrial America, geometric America, hard masculinity endowed by the lowering sky with just a suspicion of loneliness, a tear escaping the eye of a linebacker. Like precisionism, this photograph celebrates what critics of the urban landscape and today's urban preservationists would cite as a bad example: a parking lot as a thing of beauty, and even of pride in its itness. The tiny touch of feminine gentleness lent by the ever-so-slight, necklace-like curve of the wires—themselves a product of industrialism—only serves to emphasize the rigidity of the rest. The three imperfect triangles that punctuate the picture horizontally serve to emphasize the rectangularity and vertical thrust of the whole. Details of the picture add up to express its essential self-satisfied ungivingness.

As Popeye liked to say, "I y'am what I y'am."

Cathedral Church of the Incarnation, University Parkway and St. Paul Street, 1909–47, various architects

This is only one small part of the enormous cathedral originally planned. The first design came from Henry Vaughn in 1909. Ten years later Bertram Goodhue submitted a design similar to the cathedrals of New York and Washington in size, but the Maryland diocese never had the money to build it, and this English Gothic structure above a Norman crypt is no larger than the guildhall of Goodhue's plan. The design for what's there came finally from Frohman, Robb, and Little, of whom Philip Frohman was the principal architect of the Washington Cathedral.

One usually thinks of church architecture as dominating the place where it resides, for the simple reason that it usually does and so it's usually pictured that way. But when you come to think of it, there's every reason to show church architecture and nature as one. To those who believe in a supreme being, nature is God's gift to the world, and the place of worship is man's gift to God.

This photograph achieves that union, and, it may be added, in a manner rarely attempted. The trees here appear to be parting to show only a bit of the Cathedral Church of the Incarnation, but enough—window, buttress, roofline rising to cross—to summarize both its Gothic Revival architecture and its purpose. So completely has the integration of the two elements been accomplished that the trees appear to rise around the building in an architecturally protective manner, and the architecture seems a natural emanation of them.

Such an image isn't as often or as easily created as one might think. In two of the leading books of architectural photography, *Photography and Architecture: 1839–1939* (1982) and *Architecture Transformed: A History of the Photogra-* *phy of Buildings from 1839 to the Present* (1987), there is not a single picture that remotely approaches this one in showing architecture and nature in relation to one another. To be sure, the principal purpose of architectural photography has been to show the architecture front and center; but you would think that those who compiled the books might have tried to find at least one lone example of architecture and nature in perfect harmony. They didn't.

Scottish Rite Temple of Freema-
sonry, Charles and 39th streets,
1930 and after, John Russell
Pope, architect

A 1998 Pope biography by Steven McLeod Bedford ascribes
the building to Pope. A write-up
of the building produced by the
Scottish Rite Temple ascribes
the building to Clyde N. Friz, a
Baltimore architect, with Pope
as consultant. But the same
write-up states, "It is known
that the Scottish Rite Temple's
front is identical with the design
that Pope had prepared ...
earlier for the front of the Johns
Hopkins University's proposed
University Hall. That building
was not built and quite possibly
Pope had permission from
Johns Hopkins to make the
design ... available for use [by]
... the Scottish Rite Temple"
(*Architect John Russell Pope's*
Baltimore, 2004, p. 15). Since
the front of the building is the

main part of the exterior design,
that indicates that the design
can be given to Pope. Another
piece of evidence for the Pope
attribution is a drawing by Otto
R. Eggers of the building, which
was reproduced in the March
1929 issue of the magazine
The Architect. Eggers had been
an architect and the principal
draftsman of the Pope firm
since 1909, so a drawing of the
building by Eggers indicates it
was definitely a Pope design.

Is photography an art of fact or of illusion, of documentation or of artifice?
All of those, of course—you can't
pigeonhole a discipline whose practitioners have included Carleton Watkins and
Man Ray, Dorothea Lange and Cindy
Sherman. This photograph of a portion
of the Scottish Rite Temple of Freema-
sonry at Charles and 39th streets looks
straightforward enough, but it relates
to a bundle of periods and influences
and in so doing addresses the question
above.

What we can see of the building's
uppermost, entablature-like section
resembles a nineteenth-century photograph of an architectural monument
striving to combine maximum accu-
racy with maximum effect—Francis
Frith in Egypt, perhaps. But the flickering light along the lower side wall
brings to mind the soft-focus, romantic
work of the turn-of-the-century picto-
rialists such as Clarence White or
F. Holland Day, or perhaps most aptly
that aspect of the work of Edward Stei-
chen—think Flatiron Building. The
window with the air conditioner left in
celebrates the ordinary à la Walker
Evans, or maybe the ugly à la Diane
Arbus. And the shadows that, because
of the placement of the camera, appear

to be continuations of walls, create a sense of spatial ambiguity that leads to visual confusion akin to what one might experience with a Man Ray Rayograph.

What this all adds up to, however, is different from a postmodernist pastiche of derivations, though it may on some level be a satire of such. Beyond that, it's a candidate for the quintessential image of the photographer, because it coaxes the viewer to look and look, notice and notice, analyze and analyze the image—as architecture, as photograph, and as a work of art both complete in itself and resonant of other art. There's also richness here, of tone and angle no less than of allusion and illusion. And the image lends an air of dignity to a building which, except for its portico (which we don't see), is in person rather bland and foursquare. Or is it? Does the picture not so much add that layer of dignity as find it? One of the purposes of a work of art is to excite more questions than it answers.

Shoe repair shop, Cold Spring Lane and Maynadier Road (between Schenley and Hawthorne)

Can the humble be as interesting as the grand? Well, at least it can be a relief from it. As any sightseer or museum-goer knows, too much of a good thing, and certainly of an intellectually demanding thing, can cause fatigue of eye and mind, loss of concentration, even a completely irrational annoyance at whatever one's looking at.

After most of a day "doing" the city's notable architecture, it would be refreshing to come upon this view of the side of a little building on Cold Spring Lane between Roland Avenue and Charles Street. While quite modest, it has a certain degree of charm bestowed by one particular idiosyncrasy. The right-hand window is mostly covered by a sign, but its outer dimensions can be seen, and it appears to be both farther away from the door and larger in height and width than the left-hand window.

One can imagine a single person, an amateur builder, putting up this structure, perhaps with a helper but without any particular plan. Did he try for symmetry and miss? Is there some interior reason for the differences? Or did he create them on purpose to give his façade a smidgen of interest? We'll never know, but it's most satisfying to assume the last.

Hackerman House, One West Mount Vernon Place, corner of Charles and Monument streets, 1849–51, Niernsee and Neilson, architects; 1892, Charles A. Platt, renovation architect; 1989–91, James R. Grieves Associates, renovation/restoration architects

A combination of brilliant sunshine and crisp shadow makes one corner of the portico front at Hackerman House look as new as yesterday, while the darker recesses behind imply a history waiting to be told. The photograph thus perfectly summarizes the happy history of this house, in which one of the finest buildings of the nineteenth century found new usefulness in the late twentieth. Now, its beautiful interiors probably welcome more admirers in a single year than saw them in the first 140 years combined.

The house debuted in 1850, when Mount Vernon Place was coming into its own as the social centerpiece of Baltimore. J. R. Niernsee and J. C. Neilson, leading architects of mid-nineteenth-century Baltimore, designed it for Dr. and Mrs. John Hanson Thomas. The press immediately recognized its importance as townhouse architecture. The style is basically late Greek Revival, but with touches of the Italianate style then coming into vogue, such as the tall casement windows with their surmounting brackets and the heavy cornice. Originally covered with a gray stucco wash to resemble stone, the bricks were bare in recent decades, but have now been painted to resemble the original and proper appearance. The handsome double-staircase portico leads to a marble-floored hall with Corinthian columns, a classical double parlor with more columns, an Elizabethan library, and a Gothic dining room. Such eclecticism of interior design was popular at the midpoint of the nineteenth century.

Under its second owners, the Francis Jenckses, the house was somewhat "modernized" by architect Charles A. Platt. He enclosed the back porch, widened the staircase and put in a Tiffany window at the top, added a bay window to the dining room, and introduced touches in the Italian Renaissance style then popular. His work respected the overall design of the house.

It remained in private hands until the 1980s, when the third owner, Harry Gladding, moved out and left its future in doubt until developer Willard Hackerman bought it and gave it to the neighboring Walters Art Gallery (now Walters Art Museum) for restoration/renovation as a repository of Asian art. As eighteenth- and nineteenth-century owners of Chinese porcelains sometimes placed them in European ormolu mounts, so in this case a museum has placed its whole collection of Eastern art in a handsome Western setting.

The story of Hackerman House relates to the story of Mount Vernon Place. Once the neighborhood of the rich and socially prominent, its buildings have when necessary found new uses, and it continues to flourish. This picture tells the story of house and neighborhood in a single image: a survivor from a former period boldly and confidently steps into the sunlight of a different era.

Garage, 3300 block St. Paul Street, 1926, Palmer, Willis and Lamdin, architects, torn down in 2004

The walls flanking the walkway to this garage entrance on St. Paul Street just north of 33rd Street do not seem to have been added as a safety precaution, to prevent people from falling off, as the walkway is virtually on the same level as the ground on each side. It appears more likely that they were added primarily if not exclusively for an aesthetic purpose, to heighten the illusion of distance, and thus make this approach a descendant of mannerist and baroque architectural design elements created for the same purpose.

Two Italian examples come to mind. The Laurentian Library in Florence is approached by a vestibule or anteroom (1525–59 and after) by Michelangelo and Giorgio Vasari. It contains a triple staircase that becomes a single staircase as it rises, thus creating an extended sense of perspective. In addition, niches decorating the walls are topped by pediments and flanked by pilasters that taper downward to increase the illusion of height. More than a century later, Bernini's Scala Regia (1663–66) at the Vatican in Rome has much more dramatic and exaggerated perspectives.

Here we have a similar treatment. In particular, the raising of the walls as they proceed away from the viewer

and toward the doorway makes the walk seem narrower at the far end than at the near end, thus making it appear to the eye longer than it is. In addition there is an illusion of movement, of the walls rushing toward the door. This is far more modest than its Italian ancestors but pleasing in its own small way.

The Peabody Institute, Johns Hopkins University, One East Mount Vernon Place, Charles and Monument streets, 1859–66, Lind and Murdoch, architects; 1875–78, Edmund G. Lind, architect

The Peabody complex really consists of two buildings erected a decade apart but with a Renaissance Revival exterior that ties them together. The first three bays east of Charles Street, by Lind and Murdoch, contain an auditorium, a spiral metal staircase, and other rooms for the conservatory. The middle bay with portico is a one-room-deep connector to the library building, one of the finest interiors in Baltimore, by Lind: a grand hall surrounded by six stories of structural and decorative ironwork stacks. The library was an early fireproof structure of iron, tile blocks, and masonry walls and foundation.

From time to time it has been argued that the statue of Chief Justice Roger Brooke Taney—who in 1857 handed down the notorious *Dred Scott* decision upholding slavery, a decision that helped to precipitate the Civil War—should be removed from the grounds of the Maryland State House in Annapolis. Now that it has become increasingly unacceptable for southern states to fly the Confederate flag, there seems to be increasing sentiment that anything associated with a favorable attitude toward slavery should be abolished.

I do not quarrel with that opinion. I merely ask how far this kind of thinking should be carried. How far should present society go to proclaim its total rejection of a past evil? Is there a logical line someplace, on one side of which everything associated favorably with the evil should be abolished, and on the other side of which nothing should? Is there a point at which such efforts to proclaim rejection of past evils become ridiculous, or not? Is anyone who calls any effort to proclaim total rejection of past evils—no matter how extreme—ridiculous, announcing himself a racist or the like?

For instance, there is an identical statue of Justice Taney in Baltimore's

Mount Vernon Place. It isn't on state property but it's on city property. If the one at the State House should go, should the city one go too? And if so, where should they go? To someplace that isn't public property, but where they can be seen? Or should they be put permanently in storage? Or should they be destroyed? The sculpture is by William Henry Rinehart, the son of Baltimore who became an internationally recognized sculptor in the third quarter of the nineteenth century, and after whom the Rinehart School of Sculpture at the Maryland Institute College of Art is named. Should the work of a widely respected artist be destroyed?

There are also in Baltimore three monuments associated with the southern cause in the Civil War, and only one associated with the northern cause. The southern ones are the Lee-Jackson Memorial, by Laura Gardin Fraser, on Wyman Park Drive near the Baltimore Museum of Art; the Confederate Women's Monument, by J. Maxwell Miller, near the corner of University Parkway and North Charles Street; and the Confederate Soldiers and Sailors Monument, by F. Wellington Ruckstuhl, at Mount Royal Avenue and Mosher Street. Should they go, and if so where?

And what about the Washington Monument? Old George was, after all, a slaveholder.

Are we in ridiculous territory yet? If so, when did we get there? If not, should we go on? What about William Walters's collections of French academic art and Asian art, at the Walters Art Museum? William, the older of the father and son collectors, was a southern railroad owner and southern sympathizer who took his family to France in 1861 to escape the Civil War and who remained in Europe until it was over, meanwhile acquiring his collections. Should his collections not be on public view, or not be partly supported by public money, or both?

And what does this picture of the side of the Peabody Institute have to do with the subject at hand, other than, like so much else referred to here, it's on Mount Vernon Place? Look at the railing. It is in the Greek key pattern, which is nothing more than a row of swastikas connected to one another. The Webster's International Dictionary says the Greek key pattern is one of the designs "derived from or closely associated with" the swastika. The swastika is quite correctly prohibited now. But how far should the ban reach? Should this row of swastikas and all like it be replaced, or are they all right because they have a different name?

On a related issue, what about the returning of works of art and similar objects to their original owners? How far should that be carried? It seems right to return works plundered by the Nazis to the former owners or their heirs. It seems right to return stolen art or archaeological treasures to their original sites no matter whether the current owners bought them in good faith or not. But what about when they were removed by agreement with the owners at the time, but are now thought by the descendants of those owners too great a part of their heritage to allow them to stay in their present locations? Should the Elgin marbles be returned to Greece, even though the Greeks allowed them to be removed at the beginning of the nineteenth century? Should the meteorite lodged at the Museum of Natural History in New York be returned to the northwestern Indian community who want it back, even though their ancestors sold it at the beginning of the twentieth century?

No answers, just questions.

Maximilian Godefroy (1765–ca. 1838?), born and classically educated in France, immigrated to America in 1805 and came to Baltimore to live before the end of that year. He married and spent fourteen years here, from age forty to fifty-four, and they were the most productive of his life. A number of his designs no longer exist, including the Commercial and Farmers Bank and a Masonic Hall, but several have survived. The three principal ones are St. Mary's Seminary Chapel (1808), which was radically altered during its construction from Godefroy's design for the sake of economy; the Egyptian-inspired Battle Monument (1815–25); and the First Unitarian Church (1818). Of the last and most architecturally important of the three, this photograph shows the upper part of the back, the outer wall of the apse protruding in a graceful arc that complements the church's dome.

Relatively early in his Baltimore period Godefroy met and became friends with Benjamin Henry Latrobe, the great English-born architect whose now-named Basilica of the Assumption was under way during Godefroy's entire period in Baltimore. Both men's church designs are classical, and

First Unitarian Church, Charles and Franklin streets, 1818, Maximilian Godefroy, architect

The church is a cube surmounted by a hemisphere, a classic of classicism. At the front, a pedimented arcade encloses a vaulted porch. A cornice at the level of the base of the pediment extends around the building, beneath an attic story. In the pediment is a terra cotta sculpture representing the angel of truth. The original, by Antonio Capellano, sculptor of the Battle Monument also by Godefroy, deteriorated and was replaced with a replica by Henry Berge in 1954. The sides and back of the building have arched recesses, some with windows. The structure is brick covered with stucco. Originally the church nave was formed by four semicircular arches supporting the dome, the latter patterned on the Pantheon in Rome. In 1897, to improve the faulty acoustics, Joseph Evans Sperry designed a barrel vault below the dome and remodeled the interior to become a square nave and shallow side aisles formed by three arches on each side. The Godefroy pulpit remains, but the lyre-shaped organ that he also designed was replaced during the Sperry renovations. The original interior dome also remains, but now unseen above the barrel vault.

Latrobe's, much the greater, no doubt influenced Godefroy's just around the corner. In those days there was little or nothing in between, so each could be seen from the other. It is appealing to think of the architects strolling back and forth between the two in conversation, perhaps pausing somewhere near what is now the corner of Franklin and Cathedral streets to take them both in.

The beautiful triple-arched and pedimented principal façade of First Unitarian faces Franklin Street, but it is also a pleasure to see Godefroy's talents reflected in this much less often noticed portion of the rear. The church is basically a cube crowned by the half-sphere of the dome. Godefroy breaks up the mass of the cube by running a cornice around the building just at the level of the base of the pediment surmounting the entrance. The cornice breaks the walls into vertical proportions of roughly two to five, a visually pleasing relationship, and creates an upper part rising to a smaller cornice appropriate to its smaller dimensions. The upper part here appears a perfectly sized seat for the dome. The crisp corners, the

pleasing relationship between the flat ends and the rounded midsection of the upper part of the back wall, and the punctuation of this section—an indented rectangle in the curve and slits in each of the flat ends, as of a phrase between two vertical parentheses—all add up to a most satisfying architectural passage.

A master actor can often give the audience a double thrill of witnessing the total creation of a character while at the same time appreciating the skill of the actor in doing so. This photograph provides somewhat the same thrill. Part of the pleasure of seeing the architecture's virtues here comes from seeing how well they are presented. The image positions the sharp angle of the corner against the soft curve of the dome so that they interact dramatically to emphasize one another. The photographer chose a day with ideal light, one neither brightly sunny nor totally overcast. As a result, soft shadows serve to slightly heighten the emphasis of the cornices and the indentations, but one can still see every detail of each cornice, as one would not were the shadows deeper. At the same time, the darkness of the

humbler structures in the lower part of the picture, plus their placement compositionally, serve to frame and present the church's architecture to maximum advantage.

This photograph offers an opportunity to discuss the concept of sophistry, a concept it's useful to be aware of because, although it comes from ancient Greece, it's very much with us today.

The Sophists were a group of teachers in fifth-century B.C. Greece who were at first respected (especially their early leaders Protagoras and Gorgias) but later denigrated. They became known for the teaching of rhetoric (or persuasion) and political arts. They were skeptics regarding the search for truth, and some of them even deliberately practiced reasoning that was superficially convincing but essentially false. That kind of reasoning is the principal meaning that has come down to us of the word *sophistry*. (Other words deriving from *Sophist* include *sophomoric* and *sophisticate,* the latter being a term some people, who haven't looked it up, regard as a compliment.) Following is an example of what might pass for fairly basic sophistry.

Here in a hall at the main building of the Maryland Institute College of Art we have two objects (if we pay no attention to the trash can). One consists of the base, capital, and entablature of an Ionic column with the shaft missing—obviously by design and for teaching purposes, so that one can have all of the distinguishing elements of the Ionic column close enough to eye level to study them in detail. The other is the sculpture of a young woman, also created presumably for teaching purposes, which is maimed. The right arm and hand are completely gone, and the left arm and hand are damaged. Now, which of these more closely resembles the Venus de Milo, the Greek sculpture in the Louvre, which to many represents, even in its armless state, the perfection of female beauty?

The obvious answer is the sculpture of the young woman. Like the Venus, she is an example of sculpture, not architecture; she depicts the female form; she derives, if at some remove, from the ancient ideal of female beauty; and her missing parts give her one more aspect in common with Milo's sculpture. The partial column can claim none of those similarities.

The obvious answer, however, is wrong, for in essence the partial column is far closer to the Venus.

As soon as we see the partial column, we understand its study purpose and its ability to fulfill that purpose. It pleases, therefore, our sense of purpose and order, but it also pleases us aesthetically by visually declaring its aptness for the job it was intended to do. It fulfills its purpose precisely because it is not whole, for if it were whole one would have to get down close to the floor to study its base and look far up to study its capital and entablature.

We also accept the partial Venus de Milo as capable of fulfilling its purpose, to depict female beauty. In fact, most would probably say that it also fulfills its purpose better in its partial state than if it were whole, for we cannot imagine arms that would equal the beauty of what we know. In fact, there have been attempts to picture it with arms added, and they inevitably look ridiculous, or even blasphemous, for it seems that any attempt to "restore" the sculpture would be to assert the imperfection of what exists. The partial Venus does perfectly what it was intended to do, just as the partial column does.

The sculpture here of the young woman, on the other hand, violates our sense of purpose and order, for it is an imperfect teaching object as it stands. It also displeases us aesthetically, for it's unpleasant to look at in its injured state, and obviously would be more pleasant to look at if it were whole. Thus in that

sense it is the opposite of the Venus de Milo.

Therefore it is proven that the partial column more closely resembles the Venus de Milo than the sculpture of the young woman.

Now, why is the above an example of sophistry? Because the terms of the argument were changed in midstream. When the question was first put of which object seen here *more closely resembles* the Venus, that statue by Milo was immediately described as "the Greek sculpture in the Louvre, which to many represents … the perfection of female beauty." The statement implied, though it did not specifically spell out, that the comparison was to be made on the basis of physical appearance. And indeed the argument proceeded to compare the female sculpture here with the Venus in terms of physical appearance. But then the argument went off in a completely new direction, by announcing that the operative comparison would be made on the basis of certain nonphysical characteristics called "essential," thus implying that the physical comparison was merely superficial and nonessential. Such a bait-and-switch tactic is similar to this description of sophistry by Coleridge:

"The juggle of *sophistry* consists, for the most part, in using a word in one sense in the premise, and in another sense in the conclusion" (*Webster's New International Dictionary of the English Language,* 1921, p. 1995). Here, the premise leads the reader to assume that one type of comparison will be used, while the conclusion is based on a completely different type of comparison.

The bait-and-switch aspect may be classical sophistry, but in the fullness of time the word has come to have a broader dictionary definition of "specious but fallacious reasoning"— specious meaning something that appears just or correct but in reality isn't so. Thus sophistry means an argument that appears correct but is deliberately and deceitfully false.

Now, why is it important to know what sophistry is? Because it always has been and still is widely used in political discourse.

For example, those against equal rights laws for minorities at times oppose them on the basis that such laws would give whatever minority they would benefit "special rights" or "special privileges" that other people don't have. That's tantamount to saying that there shouldn't be laws against discrimination on the basis of race because such laws would give African Americans rights that white people don't have. Or that there shouldn't be laws against discrimination on the basis of sexual orientation because such laws would give homosexuals rights that heterosexuals don't have. That's a classic example of sophistry. On the surface it's a correct argument, because in fact laws against racial discrimination aren't enacted for the purpose of protecting white people, and laws against sexual discrimination aren't enacted for the purpose of protecting heterosexuals. But that's because white people aren't discriminated against on the basis of race, so they don't need such laws, and heterosexuals aren't discriminated against on the basis of sexual orientation, so they don't need such laws. It would be equally ridiculous to say that since public access laws only benefit those with physical disabilities, they give those individuals special rights that the physically able do not have. Or imagine saying that since laws allowing women to choose abortion do not apply to men, therefore they give women a special privilege. So the argument against equal rights laws on the basis of "special rights" or "special privileges" is specious—it appears correct but in reality isn't so—and thus is an example of sophistry.

It is useful to be aware of sophistry when listening to political discourse, for when it fits it tells you that the person you're listening to is trying to muddy the waters of the issue under discussion to keep people from seeing clearly.

What a mouth-wateringly delicious composition we have here.

The eating words are thrown in because the sight of this photograph of a portion of the side of Grace and St. Peter's Episcopal Church at Park Avenue and Monument Street makes one want to get one's teeth into it— almost literally, as it turns out.

An 1852 design by Baltimore's leading mid-nineteenth-century architects Niernsee and Neilson, the church is based on English rural parish architecture, with a most attractive exterior and a well-designed and outfitted interior. Its brownstone façades are gradually wearing away, as can be seen here. That's no doubt a problem for the church to deal with, but it gives the surfaces an aged, weathered, picturesque appearance that only adds to the medieval flavor. And flavor is appropriate here, because these surfaces resemble two shades of chocolate—the original striated surfaces, where remaining and darkened by the dirt of a century and a half, look like dark chocolate, and where they have flaked away the lighter brown underneath looks like milk chocolate. It makes us chocolate lovers want to get our teeth into, well, if not literally the brownstone surfaces,

This is a careful rendition of English rural parish church architecture but faced in then-popular brownstone. A planned tower above the first story on the west side was never completed. The principal interior space consists of nave and clerestory, with hammer-beam style roof trusses, wrought-iron gates on either side of the chancel, stained-glass windows (one by Tiffany), black walnut furniture, and elaborate floor tiling, much of it English.

that which they so appetizingly bring to mind.

The principal exhilaration this photograph induces, however, comes from the complex layering of parts and the surface geometries that its composition achieves. The short, square addition at the right (the sacristy), balanced by the tall chimney at left center, both attached to and in front of the side entrance, itself protruding from the apse end of the church, whose roofline is lower than that of the nave it's attached to—all of those elements make for a harmony of what architects refer to as massing, which only means how the parts are put together. Then the rectangles, the triangles, the pointed arches and round windows and roundels and trefoils of the stone tracery decoration, all add up to a geometric intricacy and a choreography of motions they imply— straight up and down, up and down at an angle, back and forth, around and around. There isn't really any motion, of course. But imagine placing this photograph on a larger sheet of paper, then extending every line that goes anywhere out a foot in each direction on the paper. Then imagine taking the photograph away and bringing all those lines back across the space where the

photograph had been. The result would probably look like a cross between geometric abstraction and Italian futurism.

There's another aspect of art here, as in other works of this photographer. Like the picture of the substructure of the Kelly Avenue bridge, or the picture of the staircase at the Maryland Institute College of Art, this is a grouping of shapes and spaces that aren't contained, that continue out of the picture frame in a dynamic way. So while the church is Gothic, the picture has a flavor of the baroque. We end as we began with a reference to taste, to which can be added that this church is very much to my taste.

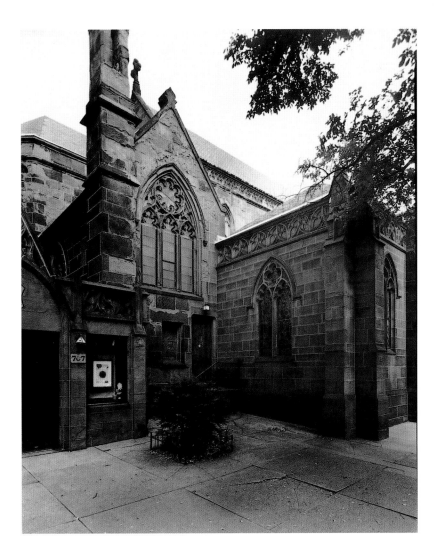

*Baltimore Museum of Art, 10
Art Museum Drive near Charles
and 31st streets. For architectural
description, see page 146.*

The empty niche, the plinth with nothing on it—one tends to think at first glance that this might be a symbol-laden scene of former glory gone. Caesar's statue removed from the senate after the assassination, or some such. But think of this image in terms of contemporary life, and it could well stand for present glory squandered. No hero stands there because we have none to put there.

The United States just now (and who knows how long it will last) is arguably the richest and most powerful nation in the history of the world, including Rome and Britain at the height of their empires. Yet internally we have enormous problems of poverty, crime, drug abuse, educational and environmental deterioration, and we don't seem to have the will to address them effectively. Externally, most of the rest of the world suffers from problems far worse than ours, but we don't seem to have the will to do more than a tiny fraction of what we might do to help.

Furthermore, and perhaps connected to our failure of will, we are at a low point in terms of artistic creativity. Our literature, our theater, our music, our fine and decorative arts, our

architecture—all were far better two and three generations ago than they are now. In fact, the first half of the twentieth century in America, as in the rest of the Western world, produced far better artists in all disciplines than did the second half, and on down to today. As a friend has trenchantly observed, we have our share of good artists, but we have no giants. Those who doubt the truth of that statement should ask themselves: Whom do we have now to equal Frank Lloyd Wright, Tennessee Williams, William Faulkner, Langston Hughes, Aaron Copland, Duke Ellington, Cole Porter, Martha Graham, Jackson Pollock, Edward Hopper, T. S. Eliot? No one. Period.

So it is in several ways appropriate that this niche at the Baltimore Museum of Art stands vacant. It reflects the present emptiness of our creativity, the failure of our leadership, and in a quite specific way the problems we address inadequately. There was never a statue in that niche, but, had there been a statue at one time, air pollution has become so destructive that it would probably have had to be taken inside, just as some years ago Rodin's *The Thinker* had to be removed from the

museum's front steps and placed inside in a space that was aptly too small for it. For *The Thinker* is heroic in stature, and apparently in this period our leaders' thinking and our nation's values are too small to produce heroes.

Rowhouses, first (unit) block East Biddle Street

New York has its skyscrapers, Chicago has its icons of modernism (whether by Sullivan or Wright or Mies), Washington has its government buildings (from the beautiful to the banal), and Baltimore has its rowhouses. My computer puts a red line under *rowhouses,* meaning it's not a word the computer recognizes. It wants me to write the term as *row houses,* which only shows that the computer was not programmed by a Baltimorean. To us, writing *row houses* is a verbal contradiction in terms, because there isn't any space between rowhouses, that's what makes them rowhouses, so there shouldn't be any space between the two parts of the word.

Rowhouses were built primarily for economic reasons. The real estate speculator could get more bang for his buck by buying a piece of land and building rowhouses on it, and the buyer could get more house for the money, especially if (as was popular at one time) he paid a ground rent rather than buying outright the land the house sat on.

But down the generations, and then the centuries, rowhouses in Baltimore have become so much more than an economic device, more even than the dominant feature of the urban land-

scape. They reflect, and maybe they even helped to form, the city's character. They are what architectural historian Phoebe Stanton called recessive, meaning the opposite of aggressive. They may have a little adornment, as this pair—in the first block of East Biddle Street built ca. 1880s—have brownstone trim and just a touch of incised decoration over the doorway, but they are visually quiet rather than loud, because that would be in bad taste. They don't want to stand out as individuals, they don't want to be noticed—or at least they don't want to *appear* to want to be noticed, because that would be vulgar.

Rowhouses also reflect the character of Baltimore in their promotion of privacy, for privacy is a condition that even the most gregarious of Baltimoreans insist upon being able to achieve when they want it. Those who inhabit rowhouses live physically close to one another, but rowhouses are actually conducive to privacy rather than community because there aren't front lawns and the back yards are often walled or fenced off from one another. Even when four blocks of rowhouses were built around a common, open square, as at Lafayette or Union Square in West Baltimore, the residents of the surrounding blocks usually look at the square from their front parlors or take individual walks in it rather than actually gather in it.

Henry James summed this up in his incomparable essay on Baltimore in the book *The American Scene,* written after his 1904 trip to his native land. He compared the Baltimore rowhouses with their protruding white stone steps out front to "rows of quiet old ladies seated, with their toes tucked-up on uniform footstools." And of the West Baltimore mini-parks he wrote, "The little ladylike squares, though below any tide-mark of fashion, were particularly frequent; in which case it was as if the virtuous dames had drawn together round a large green table, albeit to no more riotous end than that each should sit before her individual game of patience" (1968, p. 311).

This image captures the rowhouse spirit—the quietness, the uprightness, the separateness despite proximity, the restrained dignity—and bathes it in silvery light and delicate shadow. It is the only photograph of rowhouses in this book, and no other needs to be here, because this one says it all.

Here we have the other end of two rowhouse properties—not in the same location—garages facing an alley behind University Parkway in Roland Park. The University Parkway block of dwellings is largely made up of groups of three and five rowhouses, totaling twenty-two, with spaces between the groups. But they fit the rowhouse formula because the groups are arranged in a pattern—groups of 3, 5, 3, 3, 5, 3—and the fronts of each group display a uniform look. But behind the façades there can be differences, as shown here, reflecting the fact that rowhouse properties could attain a certain degree of individuality. Developers often advertised blocks of rowhouses for sale before they were built. If you contracted to buy one, certain variations were possible both inside and behind the house—as, for example, you might be able to order a larger or a smaller garage or none at all.

These "backs" appear to proclaim rowhouse individuality by their pronounced differences. The garages are different sizes. They both have impressive slate roofs, but they are of different shapes. The bond of the brick is different, the smaller garage laid in common bond (several rows of stretchers, then

a row of headers) and the larger garage laid in Flemish bond (each row alternates headers and stretchers), a high-toned bond for a garage. The doors are painted different colors. The steps from the back walkways to the alley are not quite the same. Even the telephone pole, placed exactly on the property line, seems to emphasize the separation, as does the concrete diagonal that separates the steps of the two.

Moreover, while the fronts of the twenty-two houses are in a strict pattern of groupings, there is no pattern to the garages and lack of garages, indicating that they were ordered individually according to each buyer's wish. There are seven of the smaller garages resembling the one on the right, but with variations, six of the larger garages as on the left, but also with variations, and nine properties with no garage. Starting at one end of the block there are no garages at houses number 1, 5, 7, 9, 12, 14, 18, 21, and 22. There are smaller garages at houses 3, 4, 6, 8, 13, 16, and 17. There are larger garages at houses 2, 10, 11, 15, 19, and 20. If there's a pattern there, it's more subtle than I can find.

If rowhouse façades have something to do with the character of Baltimore as a city, the differences between the uniform façades and what's behind them can reflect a complex problem of a nation of immigrants: the fact that we have triple rather than dual identity ambiguity—national, cultural, and individual—and are as a nation especially conscious of the ambiguity. On one level we want identity as Americans, we advocate and champion teamwork, our declaration of nationhood states as proudly as it does inaccurately that "all men are created equal," and our national motto, still stated on our currency in Latin, is "E Pluribus Unum"—out of many one. But at the same time each of us wants to be recognized as an individual, and in recent decades the tide of multiculturalism has drawn more and more people toward increased identity with their cultural origins, be they racial, ethnic, national, religious, or in many cases a combination of such.

Everyone, of course, has a conflict between group and individual identity, but Americans seem to be especially conscious of it because it's layered in all of us, and we are unique as a nation in having so many different kinds of layering. Thus the consciousness of identity conflict is part of our culture as Americans, and it may be the reason baseball developed as the kind of game it is. As

a sport it is the ultimate manifestation of the duality of group and individual identity, and as such it is the representation of our American ideal that different identities can coexist in harmony. Baseball's a team sport, but every member of the team has a separate and individual function, all are far enough apart that each one can be singled out for individual attention, there's no repeated bunching up together as there is in other team sports such as football and basketball and lacrosse, and a player in any position can be a star, either on offense, on defense, or both. I am aware of no other sport that so perfectly combines group and individual identity.

And coming full circle, I am aware of no other domestic living arrangement that so perfectly combines group and individual identity as the rowhouse. Whereas the stand-alone house reflects individual rather than group identity and the apartment house reflects group rather than individual identity, the rowhouse represents a synthesis of the two. It presents a façade that's part of a team, but each house presents to the world a separate entrance to an individual living unit behind the façade. So as baseball is the ultimate American sport, rowhouses

may be the ultimate American form of housing. If so, Baltimore, known better than any other American city for rowhouse living, may be the most thoroughly American of cities in terms of domestic living arrangements.

Opposite, left:
Front steps, 800 block Park Avenue

Opposite, right:
University Baptist Church, 3501 North Charles Street, 1926–28, John Russell Pope, architect

Of Pope's four complete (not partial) buildings in Baltimore (the others being the Baltimore Museum of Art, the Scottish Rite Temple, and the James Swan Frick House), this one has the most Renaissance-like feeling, with its twelve-sided dome topped by a cupola and the delicate arcade facing Charles Street. The building is one of the Pope firm's finest churches, handsome internally as well as externally; it's sited well and leaves the impression of being larger than it is.

In terms of aesthetics (the study of beauty in the arts, in the broadest sense of both words), a poet friend of mine once said, "One must always keep in mind the distinction between judgment and taste." That is to say, the distinction between what one judges on the basis of one's learning and thought to be good or bad and what one simply likes or dislikes.

It can seem a specious distinction, because if one has at least some degree of knowledge, maturity, and wisdom, is one not bound to like what one judges good and dislike what one judges bad? Well, usually, but not always, and, in relation to art about which there is an accepted body of opinion, it is usually pretty easy to know when there's a distinction.

I, for instance, dislike the music of Wagner although I know he was one of the greatest composers who ever lived. And the dislike is a reaction to the music itself, not based on any knowledge of his personality or thought. I just don't like listening to Wagner's music, and the older I get the more I dislike listening to it and the more I avoid doing so. That's purely a matter of taste, because when I do listen to it my judgment tells me it's great music.

So that's a case of taste overruling judgment on something not only good but great. On the other side of the coin, is there something I love that's inferior? Sure. I'd much rather eat a well-prepared hamburger than the choicest filet mignon.

As to the above, there's a body of accepted opinion that lets me know that, in the opinion of discriminating minds, my taste is winning out over my judgment. And I agree. My own judgment tells me the same thing.

But it can be more difficult to know the distinction in terms of the innumerable little aesthetic reactions one experiences in the course of daily life. In such cases, it is not always apparent whether one is bringing to bear one's knowledge and analytical acumen or reacting to something out of sheer bias, or to what degree each plays a part.

And here we come to the two photographs at hand, the dominant elements of which offer two differing cases in point. The curved stair railing with its thick support, ending in a round upright that looks like a misplaced ship's capstan, I find one of the ugliest examples of such an architectural detail that I can think of. No, let me make that

an absolute. I can think of none other so ugly.

And I have a similar reaction to the corbel-like decorative stone curlicue above the stair in the other picture. The picture as a whole is a beautiful composition, with its vertical, horizontal, and diagonal elements and its organic and geometric shapes all flowing out from and back to the curlicue, which acts as the centerpiece not only in terms of composition but in terms of the picture's content: in material it is like the geometrics but in shape it is like the organics. It so offends my eye, however, that for me it ruins an otherwise extraordinary picture.

I can't swear it's the ugliest such ornament in my visual experience, but it seems gross, overblown, pretentious, and even almost cartoonish, with its tongue-like excrescence protruding from the near end—a piece of pure kitsch, as distinct from schlock (that is to say, something that pretends to quality that it doesn't possess, as distinct from mere trash that has no pretensions).

In the case of the stair-rail element, I feel on pretty solid ground. I regard my opinion of its ugliness as a case of judgment. Its lumpishness and squatness, its awkward curves, its dirty color all conspire to make it a quite minor but unmistakable aesthetic disaster.

In the case of the other I'm less sure. Is it really as offensive as I find it, or is it a fairly standard, stock piece of decoration to which, out of idiosyncratic taste, I'm overreacting? And if the latter, what in my background causes the overreaction?

I just don't know. But I do know that it's worthwhile to keep the taste and judgment distinction in mind.

Sometimes architecture that's not important can be more satisfying than architecture that is.

This modest apartment building at 4300 Roland Avenue, near the Roland Park water tower, has no claim to architectural significance. It isn't a great building of its style, which is more or less Arts and Crafts. It doesn't stand as a signature building of Roland Park. It doesn't put itself forward in any way. But everything about it is so right.

Its size is right for its place—larger than a house, but not as large as the apartment buildings across the street that proceed down University Parkway and are aesthetically dull. It all fits together. The sizes of the windows in relation to one another, and their proportions and variations. The differences in the curves of the tops of the windows on the first and second floors, one softer and the other crisper. The indentation of the central section of the building, which is just right in proportion to the overall massing, and the tiny protrusion of the doorway, which complements the indentation by not trying to copy it. The slanted roof over the doorway, the one diagonal that acts as a foil for all the verticals and hori-

*4300 Roland Avenue, now con-
dominiums, date and architect
unknown (probably 1910–20,
based on the style), Edward F.
Palmer possible architect*

Palmer did a lot of work in
Roland Park at that period,
including a group of about
eighteen houses near Falls
Road and Northern Parkway,
all variations on the Arts and
Crafts style (see p. 38).

zontals. The neat decorative touches,
such as the keystone effect over the
second-floor windows and the slightly
raised concrete panels under the same
windows. The off-white color of just the
right shade, slightly soft to marry visually the angular geometry of many of
the architectural details and the curves
of others, but not soft enough to make
the whole thing look rich. Restraint is
the essential element of this architecture.

It's all extremely tailored looking
and in its own way quite chic, like a
Chanel suit. There's no misstep, there's
nothing wrong with it. It's a gem of
nonimportance, which makes it in its
own way important. We all know the
story of "Le Jongleur de Notre Dame,"
a humble man who did what he did so
well that the Virgin honored him with
a gesture she did not bestow on far
grander people. To me, this building
stands as Le Jongleur de Notre Dame of
Baltimore architecture. It's not important, but it does what it does perfectly,
and more people should notice.

*Merryman Court, Keswick Road
at Northfield Place, two blocks
south of Cold Spring Lane, 1910,
Edward L. Palmer, architect*

Of the words in the English language meaning uninhabited, the one that probably has the most negative ring is *desolate*. "Destitute, or deprived, of inhabitants," goes the dictionary definition, and also "deserted," "gloomy," "forlorn." But none of them has the hollow ring of *desolate* and its perhaps even more hollow-sounding noun, *desolation*. So it's odd that poets have not made better use of them. Probably the best use in *Bartlett's Quotations* is

*The sea, unmated creature, tired and lone,
Makes on its desolate sands eternal moan*

by one Frederick William Faber—scarcely a household name, but in this case he has done better than Shakespeare, Milton, Keats, and Poe, all of whom use the word less effectively.

In terms of art, probably the most famous work to employ the word is Thomas Cole's *Desolation* (ca. 1836), the fifth and final painting in his celebrated series "The Course of Empire," after *The Savage State, The Arcadian or Pastoral State, Consummation,* and *Destruction*. In *Desolation*, the sun sets on a scene of ruin, with vines encircling a single column in the foreground—nature reclaiming the earth from the hand of man.

In its own way this photograph is reminiscent of that painting. There are no ruins here—nothing's crumbling, nothing's even unkempt. But, pictured on what looks like a bone-chillingly raw winter's day, this unpeopled scene of roadway, wall, and bare trees possesses an overwhelming sense of emptiness and of unfelicitous silence—the silence of undesired solitude. The foreground pillar, with its head-and-shoulders-like finial, has the air of some faithful retainer, standing at endless attention, awaiting the return of a master who, we know, never will return.

Somehow, there is a feeling of Chekov about this scene, too—it might be the gateway of an estate in one of his plays in which, no matter how large the cast, a sense of individual aloneness facing some impending doom pervades.

As Roland Parkers know, this in reality is no scene of desolation but the entrance to Merryman Court, just off of Keswick Road south of Cold Spring Lane. It is an attractive square bordered on three sides by houses, which looks like a most appealing place to live. There is no overt manipulation here, but fact shown in such a light (literally) that it creates a feeling quite different

from reality. So on one level this is a quite postmodernist photograph, one that demonstrates photography can be a medium of fact but not truth, a subject to be explored at greater length in the next entry.

Venus Cleaners and Alterations, Roland Avenue and 40th Street

Eyes have been called windows of the soul, which people ordinarily take to mean that if you look into them they can show you what kind of person lies behind the façade. But it can mean the same thing in reverse. Eyes, like windows, are to be looked out of as well as into. And what the person looking out of them says about what he or she sees can be a far better indication of what lies behind the façade than merely looking into them. When one thinks of the "eye" in terms of the photograph, it all becomes extremely complicated and many-layered, as Christopher Isherwood surely knew when he wrote the ironic sentence in *The Berlin Stories* that begins with the famous words, "I am a camera" (*Goodbye to Berlin*, 1963, p. 1).

It is the full sentence that forms an example of true Socratic irony, meaning "simulation of ignorance," as it reads, "I am a camera with its shutter open, quite passive, recording, not thinking." For it is as impossible to believe that Isherwood thought that's what he was doing as it would be impossible for the photographer to characterize himself in terms of the novelist's tools by saying, "I am words, lying here on the page, signifying nothing." Lying, yes,

Sav-It Liquors Lottery, 329 West 29th Street

Opposite:
Maurice's Reupholstery, 908 South Charles Street

which is just what Isherwood was doing, for surely he knew that the novelist observes, selects, interprets, analyzes, composes, and so on and so on, just as the photographer does.

What is it that we see, then, in a photograph? Is it the object as it is, or is it the object as the photographer wants us to see it for his own purposes, which may have very little to do with the object per se, or is it the image as the viewer wants to see it, which may have very little to do with what the photographer had in mind, or is it the image in its sociological context, which may have very little to do with either photographer or viewer? Exploring the subject with half a dozen pictures of storefronts—which can also be thought of as windows to what's behind them—it turns out that there is no such thing as the object "as it is," for context is inevitable.

Klein's Hardware, 912 South Charles Street

First, a twosome in North Baltimore. Venus Cleaners and Alterations resides at Roland Avenue and 40th Street, on the southern edge of Roland Park. About ten blocks south one finds Sav-It Liquors Lottery at 329 West 29th Street in Remington. Venus looks clean, positive, well kept, a nice, respectable, thriving little business. Sav-It, with its dark and dingy front, the clumsy apparatus from which the sign hangs, its partly

dislodged and dirty-looking awning, and the front window's protective grille that brings to mind the criminal mentality, presents a dreary and depressing face to the world.

The descriptions above reflect to some extent what's there in each case. But they also have something to do with how they were photographed and presented. Venus is shown in full sunlight on a crisply clear day, and

also head-on, as if looking the viewer straight in the eye. All of that helps to suggest openness, frankness, nothing to hide. Sav-It is shown on what looks like a gray, dull day, and it's photographed at an oblique angle so that it looks as if it's not meeting the viewer's eye, and also so that one sees the ugly-looking duct work on the building next door. All of that reinforces the dark and gloomy image, the impression of shrinking away from the onlooker's gaze. Since vertical is more formal than horizontal that helps the image to look as if it's trying to keep the viewer at arm's length, as though there is something to hide.

How they were photographed, and how I see them, doubtless has something to do with our attitudes, which in turn reflect society's attitudes, toward cleaners and liquor stores. The one does something good; the other does something many regard as detrimental. It may also have something to do with the fact that Venus is located near upscale Roland Park while Sav-It is in working-class Remington. Finally, if the photographer chose to photograph these two establishments in different ways, I, not he, chose to put the photo-graphs together and compare them as I have done.

Now for a twosome in South Baltimore. Here no neighborhood prejudice can be brought to bear, since the establishments are two doors from one another at 908 and 912 South Charles Street. There's no discernible difference in the weather or the light, since sunlight seems to be evident in reflections on both front windows. The businesses are different, but while Maurice's Reupholstery may suggest a somewhat more upscale clientele than Klein's Hardware, there's no societal bias against either one, as in the case of a liquor store.

Still, there are differences. Maurice's has a neat and attractive front window occupied by a sofa and with the shop sign on a drapery-like background, suggesting a concern on the part of the shop owner to put forward an appearance that will appeal to a genteel clientele. At Klein's, one can see only a corner of the shop window, but it doesn't look as if it's dressed with any sort of display. It looks as if you see the inside of the store. The store's name is missing letters. The "Open" sign in the door has slipped, and the 912 on the

Next spread, left:
Empty shop window, 1100 block South Charles Street

Next spread, right:
Former Tiber Bookshop, 8 West 25th Street

door frame looks just stuck on rather than neatly applied. In short, not much attention to appearance here.

It's easy to infer different kinds of people behind these façades, but it also seems as if the photographer definitely guides us in that direction, indeed as if he took the pictures in order to present the contrast between them. At Maurice's, there's a presentation of the whole shop window, as if the photographer were trying his best to create a picture in keeping with the shop owner's intent. At Klein's there's only a corner of the shop window emphasizing the sloppy name sign and then about three-quarters of the picture devoted to the recess with the shop door in it. In one case, an apparently deliberately neat composition, in the other case an apparently deliberately jumbled one. The contrast here seems to me very much the photographer's and very little mine.

Finally, a pair in which one leaves everything to guesswork and the other is totally misleading. The neat and empty shop window, with its sharp clarity, its upright rather than sprawling shadows, its multiplicity of right angles, its utter cleanliness, and its orderly march of tiles below, looks like a control

freak's dream of paradise. But without a clue to go on there's no telling the location of the building or what it was, is, or will be. The photographer has achieved a quite realistic picture that is at the same time a remarkable geometric abstraction, but in terms of story the setting is bare and the scenario must be completely supplied by the viewer. After four pictures that leave the viewer uncertain about how much of what appears to be there is supplied by the photographer and how much by his or her own reaction, here is one in which everything is left to the viewer.

And then there is the Tiber Bookshop picture, in which the photographer supplies an apparently complete story, which isn't so at all. The poorly kept house, the empty window with the empty bookcase on view just inside, the signboard wretchedly besmirched with bird droppings all seem clearly to say this is a business that failed, most likely because of the ineptitude and laziness of the owners. The truth is quite the opposite. The building was at 8 West 25th Street, and when photographed was empty because it was about to be torn down along with several others to make way for the construction of a large drugstore at the corner of Charles and

25th streets. The Tiber Bookshop moved farther along the block to 24 West 25th Street, where the spotless sign and the well-stocked interior seen through the front window make it appear to be doing just fine. So any inference drawn from this picture would be totally incorrect.

To go back to where we began, the eye is no more a window on the soul than the camera is a purveyor of truth. The camera tells you what the photographer wants you to know, combined with what you make of that, and perhaps combined with the sociological context of the pictured object. The eye tells you nothing—rather the speaker's "I" tells you what the mind behind it wants you to know, combined with what you make of that. In reality, the "I" is the window of the soul, and the "I" behind the camera is the soul of photography.

The Italian Romanesque basilica as designed included a six-story tower, never completed. The brick building with light and dark sandstone trim has an appealing west front with three-arch portico and upper façade containing two relief sculptures created by Antonio Capellano for the 1817 church and saved from the 1854 fire. Inside, four arches on each side of the nave separate it from the side aisles, but the space is so open that it has the feel of a single large rectangle. Above is a clerestory with stained-glass windows. Some of the church's windows are by Tiffany, and the commanding east window over the altar is by New York's Maitland, Armstrong & Co., a Tiffany protégé.

Anyone who has looked into the subject of Baltimore architecture will know something about St. Paul's Episcopal Church at the corner of Charles and Saratoga streets, locally known as Old St. Paul's because its origins go all the way back to 1729 and thus to the very beginning of Baltimore. The present, fourth building, dating to 1856 and designed by Richard Upjohn as an Italian Romanesque basilica, has a well-known Charles Street façade with triple-arched portico and unfinished bell tower. But how many to whom the façade is as familiar as that of any church in Baltimore have bothered to look around the corner at the Saratoga Street side?

Yes, it's just "the side of the church," a working part that isn't supposed to make an aesthetic statement like the front. But look how much interest there is in this small section here presented for scrutiny. A bit of the church's history helps the looking, for the third church, designed by native Baltimore architect Robert Cary Long Sr. and opened in 1817, burned in 1854. Upjohn incorporated the foundation and the surviving brick walls of the older church, 25 to 35 feet high, into his design.

That would suggest that all of the walls we see here date to Long, but that couldn't very well be the case. The bell tower, of which the back corner shows at right, was not a feature of Long's church, and also looks all of a piece, so that part is surely Upjohn. The arched window and door openings on the ground floor look much more like 1854 than 1817, suggesting that this one-story section might be an Upjohn addition. Were the windows placed in larger blind arches purely for added architectural interest, or was it to make the addition have something in common with the blind arch above, which could possibly have been the top of a window in the Long church, closed off by Upjohn? The fact that the brickwork to the left in the upper section looks much younger lends credence to such a surmise.

But then the brickwork of the protruding first-floor section looks much closer in color to the apparently older brickwork above, resulting in some confusion. Adding to the confusion is the fact that all of the second-story brickwork, except for that of the little chimney-like vertical, is laid in Flemish bond with alternating headers and stretchers, while all of the first-floor brickwork, like that of the bell tower, is in common bond, in which courses of

stretchers are interrupted at intervals by courses of headers.

Shall we make it even more confusing? The courses of headers in the bell tower come at intervals of six, while those in the one-story addition come at intervals of eight. That might be because the brickwork in the one-story addition doesn't have as much to support as that in the bell tower, and six-course intervals of headers give greater stability than eight-course intervals. And eight-course intervals might be a little cheaper than six-course intervals. But could the savings have been that much on the one-story section we see here?

At any rate this picture provides a lot more food for looking and thinking than one would guess at a glance. And it's probable that the vast majority of people have never given this part of the church more than a glance until this photograph singled it out for notice.

House, Roland Park, between Roland Avenue and Charles Street

The tripartite opening, seen in this richly toned and softly geometric image, has been repeatedly popular throughout the history of architecture. It can take a variety of forms—a door with windows on either side, windows of varying sizes and shapes—but the three-part opening gives a sense of satisfaction and, as we shall see, identity.

Through the centuries the tripartite opening has had several periods of especial popularity. Proceeding backward, there was the period at the turn of the twentieth century (to which this example belongs) known in America and England as the Arts and Crafts period (for Arts and Crafts, see also p. 38). In that period the tripartite motif probably found its most creative advocate in the person of Viennese architect Otto Wagner. In his Postparkasse (postal savings bank, 1904–6), the triple windows over a row of doors in the main hall have a gently curving top with "shoulders" on both ends that slope into vertical sides. Elsewhere, his tripartite motifs include the continuous half-round arch and variations—some might even say distortions—of the Palladian motif with arched central section and rectangular side panels.

A century earlier, during the Ameri-

can Federal period of architecture, the tripartite form was also quite popular. A form of the rectangular three-part opening with all segments of equal height, as seen here, was used for the second- and third-floor windows of a row of houses in the unit block of East Hamilton Street, between Charles and Cathedral streets, built about 1815. Baltimore architect Robert Cary Long Sr., who designed Davidge Hall and the Peale Museum, owned the Hamilton Street block and lived in one of the houses ca. 1815, so he is thought to have designed them. The half-round triple window can be seen on the side of the Carroll Mansion of ca. 1812, not far from the Inner Harbor, and also on the garden façade of the former country house Mount Clare, in southwest Baltimore's Carroll Park. Mount Clare was actually built in the colonial period, and originally had a round window in the triple window's location. In 1787, when the Federal period was taking hold, Margaret Tilghman Carroll, the widow of builder Charles Carroll, Barrister, had the window changed to half-round triple form among other changes in keeping with the latest style. And at Homewood, the greatest Federal building in Baltimore and one of the greatest

in the United States, there are no fewer than four Palladian windows in the two hyphens on the front façade, plus Palladian variations in three doorway treatments (two exterior, one interior).

The Palladian motif was popularized in the sixteenth century by the Italian Antonio Palladio (1508–80), perhaps the most influential architect in history because of his own buildings plus his four-volume treatise *The Four Books of Architecture*. The Palladian motif, as indicated above, is an arched central section flanked by two lower rectangular openings. Palladio used repetitions of it to form the façades of his first public commission, the architectural "envelope" he designed for the Palazzo della Ragione, or Basilica, an already standing municipal building in the town square of Vicenza. The Palladian motif's form had actually been published earlier, in a print of 1537, by another architect, Sebastiano Serlio, so some purists call the form the Serlian motif or serliana. But Palladio was so much more influential as an architect that the form is overwhelmingly associated with his name. And not wrongly so, since Serlio's form was itself not a totally original innovation but based on a much older form.

One of the most popular works at the Walters Art Museum is a painting, of 1490–1500 by an anonymous artist, called *View of an Ideal City*. In it, facing the viewer across a grand plaza, are three structures, representing the Colosseum, the Baptistry in Florence, and a triumphal arch (in the center). According to the entry accompanying a photograph of the painting in a Walters publication, these represent "three main aspects of communal life: military, recreational, spiritual" (*The Walters Art Gallery Guide to the Collections,* 1997, p. 51). The triumphal arch, of course, represents the military, and in the painting it is a structure with three arches, the middle one wider and higher than the side ones. Thus the origin of the Palladian motif was the triumphal arch that goes back to Roman times, when it memorialized a military triumph. Roman triumphal arches had either one or three arched openings, the best known of the latter type being the arches of Septimius Severus (A.D. 203) and Constantine (A.D. 312) in Rome. According to architectural historian Sir Banister Fletcher, in the three-arched version, the side arches were footways. (Fletcher does not specify it, but the central arch must

have been for cavalry and the chariot that bore the triumph's hero.) These triumphal arches, Fletcher writes, "first occur about 200 B.C., but few now surviving are much earlier than the reign of Augustus" (*A History of Architecture,* 1963, p. 221).

The three-opening triumphal arch thus had a utilitarian purpose, as doors and windows do. But the major status of the tripartite opening in architecture probably stems from more than usefulness, principally two other causes. First, three is the smallest symmetrical grouping centered on a single unit. Second, and perhaps more important, the tripartite opening is anthropomorphic. The equally tall triple opening in the photograph opposite and even more so the sloping, "shouldered" triple opening in Wagner's Postparkasse, resemble the human torso and arms. The Palladian motif and triple-opening triumphal arch, in which the central section is considerably higher and rounded, resemble the torso and arms crowned by the head. One theme of this book is to demonstrate how we all relate to the history of civilization, and we could not relate more basically than we do to the tripartite architectural opening.

*Building, 900 block South
Charles Street*

Some things you don't want to know.

It is possible to know a little and deduce a little more about what's in this picture by looking at it. The building dates from the first half of the nineteenth century, as indicated by its pitched roof and its square third-floor windows. The size of the front part of the house and its modest windows with their wooden lintels and sills indicates that it was originally in a middle-class neighborhood, and its commercial first floor suggests that that's still the case. The sun shining full force on the façade suggests that the building doesn't face north, a conjecture supported by the angles of the shadows in the windows.

There is no Lorad … Construction company listed in the current telephone book, so the company has probably either gone out of business or moved out of the metropolitan area. The 783 exchange in the 410 area code is a Baltimore city exchange, but it seems a pretty rare one. Since exchanges are largely geographical, I looked through pages in both the residential and commercial phone books for another 783 number to which an address was attached and had to look down 28¾ columns, or

roughly 1,700 telephone numbers, before finding one with the 783 exchange. The address was Battery Avenue, which runs up Federal Hill, so this building is likely to be in South Baltimore.

That much can be found out through an examination of the picture. But something else can't. What about those nine bands of light on the side wall? Yes, they are light, not white paint. That becomes evident if you look at where they fall across parts of the building's windows and lighten them. But how on earth are they created? Even if the sun were shining through something such as openings in a wall, it would be difficult to imagine what kind of openings and what kind of a wall, because the shapes are not like those of windows. But the sun is coming from the other direction. Nor is it likely to be bouncing off of windows in a neighboring building, since again the patches of light are not window-shaped.

My best guess, after looking at this picture for a long time, is that the sun is bouncing off of some strips of shiny, reflective metal on a neighboring wall. It's hard to imagine why such strips would be there, but no more plausible possibility suggests itself so far.

Perhaps one will someday, but I shall never ask the photographer for the answer to this puzzling image. It's much more fun to conjecture every time I see the picture than it would be to know. The effect is magical, mysterious, and compelling.

Walters Art Museum Centre Street Building, Centre and Cathedral streets, 1974, Shepley, Bulfinch, Richardson and Abbott, with Meyer, Ayers and Saint, architects; 1999–2001 renovation, Kallmann, McKinnell, Wood, architects

This addition to the Walters attempted to be both larger than the original building and modern in style but visually in keeping with the original 1905 building. It succeeded in some ways: on the exterior it's visually compatible in mass and height, with the same cornice line, while on the interior it has six floors compared to the original building's three, and in terms of square feet it is about twice the size of the original building without looking larger from the exterior. But aesthetically the Brutalist exterior is out of keeping with the 1905 structure and in general forbidding, and the interior was originally confusing and gloomy. A $25 million renovation and reinstallation with a reopening in 2001 improved the interior greatly and in effect did away with its problems. Despite a dramatic new entrance, the exterior is still off-putting, and no doubt always will be, but the interior is much the more important aspect of the building.

Brutalism, the word, entered the language in the 1950s as the title of a style of high modern architecture characterized by massive, sometimes rough, largely blank, and often hostile-looking concrete walls. (The more general noun derived from the word brutal is of course brutality, and refers to conduct. The term *Brutalism,* and the corresponding adjective *Brutalist,* refer only to the architecture style.)

Among Brutalism's leading practitioners were Le Corbusier of France, Alison and Peter Smithson of Britain, and Paul Rudolph of the United States, and the style lasted for about thirty years. At its best, as with Rudolph's art and architecture building at Yale or Corbusier's Chandigarh complex in India, Brutalism could achieve a dignified monumentality. But it was more often simply forbidding-looking, and could be especially unfortunate when employed for the design of public buildings, which frequently ended up looking like fortresses defending themselves against the very people they were supposed to welcome.

Such is more or less true of the two principal Baltimore buildings revealing Brutalist tendencies: less so of John Johansen's Mechanic Theater of 1967 in Charles Center, and more so of

this, the Walters Art Museum's Centre Street Building, 1974, by Shepley, Bulfinch, Richardson, and Abbott of Boston with Meyer, Ayers, and Saint of Baltimore. As originally designed it was grossly unwelcoming inside as well as outside, with its depressing entrance hall, gloomy and confusingly laid-out galleries, and dungeon-like stairways. The interior was greatly improved by a recent $25 million renovation, and is now much more welcoming, much less confusing, and not at all gloomy. But the exterior walls remain much the same, including the fact that the one seen here could even be physically harmful to the passer-by. Those two bicycle racks were never intended for bicycles, but were put there to prevent people from bumping their heads on the bottom of the protruding wall, which at that point descends to less than 6 feet above the sidewalk.

Except in an unusual case such as this, where the wall could possibly harm someone, Brutalism has always seemed to me something of a misnomer. *Brutal,* from which it comes, means savage, coarse, cruel; all are negative words connoting a physically active role. *Bleak,* on the other hand, means desolate, cold, cheerless, depressing. They are equally negative words, but bleak is more physically passive (though to be sure emotionally active) in its connotations. Think of "Ah, distinctly I remember it was in the bleak December" (Poe) (*The Works of Edgar Allan Poe,* no date, Part III, p. 9) or "When true hearts lie wither'd / And fond ones are flown, / Oh, who would inhabit / This bleak world alone?" (Thomas Moore) (*Familiar Quotations by John Bartlett,* 1955, p. 439).

So I propose the term Brutalism be discarded in favor of Bleakism, with of course every confidence that it will immediately come to pass.

This photograph of stonework defining a black opening with no visual escape—no horizon, no sky, no nature, nothing human or forgiving—relates to the character of Brutalism as an architectural style: massive, gray, unwelcoming. And it leads one to think prison, fortress, dungeon. In fact, the building this picture comes from neither serves a brutal purpose nor stands as an example of Brutalist architecture. The doorway here leads into the Clarence M. Mitchell, Jr. Courthouse at 100 North Calvert Street. One can sometimes accurately accuse courts of brutality, but they exist to dispense justice, and in our country they do that more often than not. Architecturally, the 1900 courthouse by the local firm of Wyatt and Nolting is in the Renaissance Revival style—and renaissance stands for humanism.

But if one considers the history of Western art and architecture over the past 250 years, one can see this picture as capturing the historical subtext of this building in a way that the architects never intended or foresaw—they couldn't have. Most people agree that art reflects its period of history; fewer would agree that it foretells the future. But it is possible to interpret the history of art and architecture since 1750 in

such a way that this photograph, taken a century after the courthouse opened, embodies its foreshadowing aspect.

The premise here is that periods of relative peace and prosperity without catastrophic upheavals produce either no dominant style or a style that's diffuse, unfocused, busy, frivolous, or simply weak. But seen in hindsight, when a period of crisis and bloodshed that will change the world is about to happen, the arts take on greater seriousness and strength. This is a signal, if people could only see it, that their world will go into a period of great turmoil and change in unimaginable ways.

Let us go back to about 1780. The period of the baroque had found its final flourish in the Rococo, a style of great artificiality especially associated with France and typified by the furniture style of Louis Quinze and the art of Boucher and Fragonard. All was airiness and curlicues, love and luxury played out against a background of poverty nowhere acknowledged. But by the 1780s a new classicism arrived, sober, grounded in antiquity, more serious. For a contrast between the two, think of *The Swing* (1767) by Fragonard and *The Oath of the Horatii* (1784) by Jacques-Louis David. As some who rightly

The local firm won a national competition for design of the courthouse over such leading names as McKim, Mead and White; Burnham and Atwood; and Carrere and Hastings. The impressive building is in the ca. 1900 Renaissance Revival style, made of Woodstock granite below and Beaver Dam marble above. The Calvert Street main façade has a loggia with eight huge marble monolith columns (reportedly the largest in the world, each more than 31 feet tall and weighing 35 tons). The splendid interior was remodeled in the 1950s, when some of its best features were lost, but a number of them have been recaptured in succeeding renovations. Among the finest present spaces are the ornate former Orphans Court and the Criminal Courts lobby on the second floor, the ceremonial Courtroom 400 on the fourth floor, the Supreme Bench Courtroom and the Bar Library on the sixth floor. The building also contains murals by John La Farge, Edwin H. Blashfield, and others.

associate David with Napoleon may not know, he and the Classical Revival appeared *before* the French Revolution initiated a quarter century of European war and upheaval.

During that period, the Classical Revival reached its height (think Empire style), then declined and by mid-nineteenth century was replaced by eclectic Victorianism. With the exception of the American Civil War, the nineteenth century was on the whole without cataclysmic upheavals, though the Industrial Revolution stoked a volcano that erupted intermittently. In architecture and decorative arts, styles came and went: Rococo Revival, Renaissance Revival, Gothic Revival, Elizabethan Revival. In art, romanticism produced some great masters (Turner, Delacroix) amid a mess of mush, gush, and slush (music fared better), and academicism grew increasingly meaningless. Decoration took precedence over substance.

As the century went on, many different kinds of developments all reflected a change in tone. Whether one thinks of Manet, Monet, Cezanne, and the beginnings of modernism; the realism of Homer and Eakins; Ibsen, Shaw, and the beginnings of modern theater; the Romanesque architecture style of H. H. Richardson; or the Renaissance Revival

of century's end that was more authentic (and as this photograph shows more sturdy) than that of mid-century, they had in common great seriousness of purpose. Uh-oh.

Once again, changes in art preceded upheaval, for this building debuted with a century whose first half included World War I, the Russian Revolution, the Depression, the rise of fascism, the triumphs of Mussolini, Stalin, Hitler, and Franco, World War II, and the Holocaust. The same period saw the triumph of modernism in all forms, including art, architecture, literature, music, and theater, and it came out of World War II at its height. But that did not last long after the period of upheaval. It was soon challenged by a host of movements from pop to deconstructivism, which, in the last half century, have stormed the barricades of modernism and reduced the arts to a cacophony of whimpers.

Is this bad? Aesthetically speaking, yes. But it goes with a period of relative peace and prosperity, like Victorian revivalism and Rococo artificiality. Many of us long for a strong, fine style of substance and vigor to sweep aside all the little nonentities that pass for art today and once again provide a dominant force in the art world.

But when it arrives, beware.

Evergreen, 4545 North Charles Street, 1857–58, architect unknown; 1885, Charles L. Carson; 1922–41, Laurence Hall Fowler

The original house is the roughly cube-shaped building to which the portico offers entrance. In 1885 Carson designed for T. Harrison Garrett a north wing connected to the house by a bridge-like section that also forms a porte cochere for the service entrance. The north wing originally housed a bowling alley, gymnasium, and study rooms for the Garrett children. In 1920 T. Harrison's son diplomat John Work Garrett and his wife, art patron Alice Warder Garrett, inherited the house and for the next twenty years had it altered and added to by Fowler. In the 1920s the north wing became rooms for the Garretts' collection of East Asian art and a theater with ceiling and wall designs by Ballets Russes costume and set designer Leon Bakst. In 1928 the rare book library was added to the rear of the main house, with additional alterations to the room leading into it in the 1930s. In 1941 the double parlor became a single parlor and a small book room off of the parlor became the last addition. In 1942 Mr. Garrett died and left the property and collections to Hopkins, though Mrs. Garrett continued to live there until her death a decade later.

During the 1850s, when the South was enjoying its height of prosperity in the antebellum King Cotton slaveholding years, some of the wealthiest plantation owners built mansions in the classical style with grand-columned two-story porticos or porches, such as Waverley, of 1852, at Columbus, Mississippi. Baltimore is too far north for cotton growing, and whether the Broadbent family, who built Evergreen in 1857–58, owned slaves is not known by me. Nor is there a documented name for the architect of the original house. Evergreen, in the very late Classical Revival style with Italianate touches such as the heavy cornice and bracketed windows, definitely has a grandiose, plantation-manse feel to it.

The two-story, Corinthian-columned portico approached by a stairway of almost portico width is awkward if analyzed aesthetically. Its depth is too shallow for its height, and the columns are out of scale in relation to the structure as a whole. But it serves its purpose to impress—in spades. One approaches it at an angle, going up the driveway to where it sits on a slight rise from Charles Street. One cannot see it until one is through the gates and headed up the drive when it appears,

and when that happens it's a thrilling moment—it brings to my mind the opening of the triumphal march from *Aida*. Neither one is anything like the ultimate expression of its art, but they're both exhilarating.

This photograph, with its dramatic contrasts of light and dark, its suggestions of grandeur and decay, reflects what happened to the Broadbents soon after Evergreen was built. They went broke. They had to sell it. Like the South, they overreached. Fortunately, in 1878, after a succession of owners but when it was only two decades old, Evergreen became the property of the Garrett family. They preserved and enlarged it, lived there for three-quarters of a century, and left it to the Johns Hopkins University, which has preserved it for more than another half century. Between 1986 and 1991 the house was renovated structurally and mechanically and restored architecturally and decoratively—but not to any particular period or style. It reflects the living, collecting, and altering that went on for almost a century, and so in terms of house museums it's unusual, a breath of fresh air.

Culvert, Overhill Road between Linkwood Road and Northfield Place

This is a culvert, than which there is probably no less romantic word in the language, either in sound or in meaning. "A transverse drain under a road … " begins the dictionary definition, perfectly describing this functional bit of construction that carries Stony Run under Overhill Road on its way to Wyman Park. Yet this photograph is not about the culvert, or the bridge or the stream or the trees or anything one would likely list if asked to name what one sees in this picture. Look again.

The retaining wall at left center draws the eye down toward a bit of water meandering lazily along, but a hint of a breeze has pulled the water at lower right out of focus. In the foreground, the air is moving a little, but not much. In the background, on the other side of the bridge, the silver-gray foliage of trees looks buffeted about by a storm, and dissolves into white in the distance as if veiled by rain about to overtake the whole scene. But in the middle distance, represented by the bridge itself and the dark-leafed branches on either side, there appears to be utter calm. Every single leaf stands out with complete clarity, attesting to the total stillness of the air that appears to move gently on this side of that stillness and violently

on the other side. Is this a dream or a movie? It seems to surrealistically violate the order one naturally wishes to impose upon the scene. That's because what's actually happened here is that the photographer has made the invisible visible. He has made us see the air, a feat so rare that the poet Julia Randall once wrote about it in homage to another artist:

Vermeer could paint the light, Rembrandt
  the dark,
Whistler the fog, and several the flesh,
the fur (though mostly workshop), and
  the face
(as Velasquez), occasion, race
(as Delacroix), the endless
varieties of fruit and forest. Go
to the Hermitage. There
they stack them layer on layer,
dead rabbits and dead fish. Only Corot
could paint the air.

And maybe only DuSel can photograph the air.

Hayward-Maxwell family mausoleum, Green Mount Cemetery, 1501 Greenmount Avenue, ca. 1909, architect unknown

The mausoleum was built by two sisters of the Hayward family, Mabel Hayward Boyden and Ella Hayward Maxwell, and the first person interred there was their father, Thomas Jonas Hayward, 1847–1909, thus giving a date or near date for the building. But the date is also appropriate to the popularity of Classical Revival architecture at the turn of the twentieth century. Neither the current owner of the mausoleum nor Green Mount Cemetery has information on the architect.

Are you an optimist or a pessimist, a person with a tendency to positive or negative thought, a glass-is-half-full or a glass-is-half-empty person, generous or mean of spirit? Most of us would like to be on the sunny side of all those dualities, but if you'd like to test yourself, answer this question: What do you think of when you see this picture of a family mausoleum in Green Mount Cemetery?

Inevitably, and naturally, you think of death and the brevity of life. But beyond that, if you are by nature negative, your thoughts may go something like this: what conceit, what vanity it was of whoever commissioned this building for himself and his family to lie in when they were dead.* What a waste of money that could have been

*A pessimistic surmise that someone had it built for his glory is wrong. His daughters had it built. Another surmise, that not long after the death of the original person interred here the family would have forgotten and no longer visit, is also wrong. Throughout the century over a dozen more interments of three generations of those descended from the Hayward and Maxwell families have taken place, and there is still space for a few more. The latest was that of Aurine Boyden Morsell, 1909–94. Her daughter, Mary H. Miller, the person responsible for the mausoleum in the present generation, has made repairs and sees to its upkeep. So, encouragingly, the pessimistic would be less accurate than the optimistic assessment.

better spent in some less selfish way. And what did he do it for? So that even in death he would be housed behind a façade of grandeur for the world to admire. So that the family would come and pay him homage at this temple of death. How futile—for in a few years no one outside the family will know who lies buried there, and in a relatively few more years in the life of the world no one at all will know, or care, or come. As Thackeray wrote in *Vanity Fair*, at the end of a memorable passage on death, "However much you may be mourned, your widow will like to have her weeds neatly made; the cook will send or come up to ask about dinner; the survivors will soon bear to look at your picture over the mantelpiece, which will presently be deposed from the place of honour, to make way for the portrait of the son who reigns" (*The Limits of Art,* 1948, p. 1232).

If, on the other hand, your thoughts run positively, you may think: What a handsome little building. It's reminiscent of the McKim Free School, on East Baltimore Street, one of the best local examples of Greek Doric architecture, said to have been modeled on the Temple of Haephaestus on the Acropolis in Athens. Like McKim, this is really a

hexastyle (a fancy way of saying six-column-width) front, with the two middle ones omitted; if you measure, there's just about room for them, but of course they had to be omitted so coffins could get in. Aside from being smaller, it's a little simpler than McKim; it has an architrave (the band over the column capitals) and pediment, but unlike McKim it has no frieze between them, and it has plain rather than fluted columns. It's handsome, however, with good proportions and a fine pair of doors, and the two urns in front of the end columns add an extra touch of elegance. The laurel wreaths in the upper part of the doors surround the initials HM.

It would be nice to think that one's thoughts are apt to run along the lines of the paragraph immediately above, but mine ran along those of the paragraph preceding it until I forced them along a different path. Oh well, we can't all be Pollyannas. What about you?

This post reminds me of my parents' generation, even though it's probably older than they were—but let's look at it as a post first. It stands at the entrance to a driveway in the 4100 block of Roland Avenue. It was never meant to be an important marker. Compared to a gateway, such as the one at the northern end of Madison Avenue at the entrance to Druid Hill Park, this post is fairly far down on the scale of importance of what we might call ceremonial structures. Nevertheless, it's well made of stone, and nicely decorated with panels on the three protruding bands positioned in relation to segments of the body—the chest, the waist, the knees. Like many structures, from columns to skyscrapers, this one can be seen as anthropomorphic; it also has a shoulder and neck, though no finial representing a head, and at the bottom puts out a round foot. It probably dates from the late nineteenth century, at any rate before World War I, and although it's showing signs of age—one corner of the shoulder has become dislocated and may by now have fallen off (the picture dates from 1997)—it's still handsomer than later versions of such modest markers, which, if made at all, would at best have been of brick and more likely of concrete. Even the dirt on the post is a felicitous element in this photograph: it contributes to the rich tonality of the image. And the object's proud uprightness suggests such virtues as integrity, rectitude, and, largely because of the front-placed (as if striding) foot, determination and force of personality.

That's where my parents' generation comes in. Born in 1902 and 1904, my parents belonged to the generation of turn-of-the-century children (born around 1900) who, by the time they reached a half century or so, had lived through two World Wars and the Great Depression. The immense turmoil of the first half of the twentieth century killed many and ruined many others. But those who survived intact, at least in my experience, tended to be more full of character, more vivid of personality, and more capable of having fun than my generation. Maybe the last was because when they were young their lives contained so much strife that they needed fun more, and when it was possible they threw themselves into it. In fact, they tended to do whatever they did wholeheartedly, probably because, when struggle has been a large component of your life, you know you have to give it your all if you're going to have any chance of coming through okay. In contrast, the people of my generation, who grew up about mid-century, have had comparatively easier but duller lives, and as a natural enough result tend to be duller people.

When my parents were married, at the depth of the Depression in 1933, my father-to-be was a reporter on the Baltimore *Evening Sun,* making $18.75 a week. My mother-to-be was a nurse at the old Hospital for the Women of Maryland in Bolton Hill, working twelve hours a day, six days a week, for $60 a month—multiply and divide it out and it comes to about 20 cents an hour. Of course things were a lot less expensive then, but my parents were poor. And although both had had relatives who were better off, and were never in danger of actual destitution, they had both grown up fairly poor. I'm glad I didn't grow up poor and had the advantages I had, but I don't have the guts, the courage, the vitality and enthusiasm that they had. And neither, on the whole, does the rest of my generation. We don't, you know. It's no use protesting, we just don't, and those who remember my parents' generation will recognize that, even if they don't acknowledge it. Just as the first half of the twentieth century produced better arts than the second half, it produced better people, too.

They were formed of better stuff than we, just as this post is formed of better stuff than its descendants, and that's why it reminds me of that generation.

Art changes. It can change in many ways. Architecture changes with the weather, for instance. Works on paper change with exposure to light. Those are two different kinds of change—the first is a temporary change in the way something looks, as you look different when you change from a bathing suit into evening clothes. The second is a permanent change in a work of art's physical properties, as you change as you grow older.

A work of art, like a person, undergoes changes throughout its life, from momentary to permanent, but this text will deal with only one kind of change with two complementary aspects: how art changes people who think about it, and how people thinking about it changes art. That is the argument of this essay and this book.

The photographs seen here are images that the photographer has made different-sized prints of at different times. He made larger prints for this book. Several years ago, smaller prints of these two images were among a series of images he sent as postcards. The series was called "Look Again!"

The photographer sent the series of postcards to various people with more than one purpose in mind. In part, it was to get people to look at his photographs (a variation of a gallery exhibition), and by extension to make them curious about the guy who took the photographs, whose name and address appeared on the back of each postcard. But primarily it was to get people to look at, and think about, a detail or aspect of a work of local architecture that they may not have noticed before, or which they might be so familiar with that they never notice it anymore.

There are differences between the larger image made for this book and the smaller image sent as postcards. Art changes. One is larger than the other, and in each case the larger print is lighter in tone, and that plus the larger size makes details easier to see. The difference in size was obviously planned by the artist. The difference in tone may have been planned by the artist or may have resulted from his having less control over the printing of the postcards. In any case, it's reasonable to infer that the larger print must be taken as closer to the artist's vision, since that is the print he selected for this book. But that's wrong. He prefers the smaller print in both cases.

Also interesting to me are differences I perceive that don't really exist but that play a role in forming my responses to the two versions. In the photograph of the building, it appears to me to be at less of an angle, more flat, in the larger version, while the building in the smaller version appears to recede at a sharper angle. And the stairs appear to me more horizontal in the larger version, more vertical in the smaller. Neither is the case, of course. Similarly, in the photograph I call *Three Trees,* because it recalls Rembrandt's etching of that name, the two walls appear to meet at a sharper angle in the smaller version. In both cases, I prefer the smaller version. The smaller prints to me have more drama because the angles appear more acute.

That's accentuated by the added darkness, which gives them a slightly ominous, more emotionally charged look. In addition, the darker clouds at the top of the smaller *Three Trees* makes the composition of the print appear more balanced than that of the larger one.

Are my reasons for preferring the smaller versions similar to those of the artist? I have no idea, nor do I intend to ask, nor does the artist think it necessary to tell me. The artist who wants to explain his art to the critic is often trying to keep the critic from noticing that it's not very good. And the critic who wants the artist to explain his work often feels himself incapable of perceptive thought about it. When the artist who wants to explain his work finds the critic who wants him to explain it, you often have a meeting of two failures. It is the critic's job to notice what matters to him, not to sop up and repeat what matters to the artist.

In works of art that can be produced in multiples, such as prints and photographs, the artist can cause and the recipient can perceive change. In the case of the unique work of fine art—assuming the artist is dead or has no intention of changing it—it may seem that only the viewer's mind can change the work. That is not absolutely the case. Accidents happen. Vandalism happens. Dirt happens. Cleaning and restoration, sometimes overcleaning and overrestoration, also happen. But more often, in an age when we tend to see works first in reproduction, seeing the work itself can change the work.

Take the example of my meeting with Manet's painting *Olympia* a few years ago at the Musee d'Orsay in Paris. I had never before seen the original, but had seen it scores, perhaps hundreds,

Valve house, Society for the Prevention of Cruelty to Animals property, 3300 Falls Road, James Slade, designer

Opened in 1862, Baltimore's first publicly built and owned water supply system ran from Lake Roland in Baltimore County to the Hampden reservoir, with conduits beyond. At the two ends are valve/gate houses (containing valves controlling gates). The buildings are Greek Revival designs. The photograph is of the Hampden building, labeled "Hampden Reservoir, 1861." Both of the small buildings, with pediments at both ends, have quoins at corners and flanking end doors and side windows. Slade, a civil engineer who planned the system, is designated designer of the Lake Roland building, identical to this. An even smaller valve/gate house from 1860 stands near the Cross Keys community gatehouse in the 5100 block of Falls Road (see p. 173). It is not documented to Slade but can certainly be attributed to him based on the others. The system closed in 1915.

of times in reproduction. And in reproduction the nude woman presented as a prostitute had always seemed to me both calculating, with her narrow eyes, and defiant in her pose, with hand clamped down on her genitals, feet with boudoir mules, and head raised to stare us straight in the face. "You want my body," she seems to say to prospective clients. "Pay for it." And to the respectable bourgeoisie (who disapproved of her in part because they knew she made her living off of their class) she seems to be saying, "You don't like me? Good. Screw you. Your men screw me."

So coming upon her at the Orsay was something of a surprise, because although in the painting she appears bold even today (and always will, I think), she doesn't appear defiant. Her pose appears simply matter-of-fact. "Here I am," she seems to say, "I'm a fact of life." That is not a minor difference in terms of the painting's meaning.

Why, I wondered, does she seem so much milder in person than in reproduction? Perhaps it's partly because in books and catalogues she's reproduced on shiny paper, which can make the image harder-looking. And perhaps partly because in the presence of the painting one notices the brushstroke more than in a reproduction. So one's attention is more occupied by the fact that the artist's sensibility has fashioned this image. This is the artist's concept of how he wants to present the woman, not the woman's concept of herself.

Art history tells us that Titian's *Venus of Urbino* and Ingres's nudes influenced Manet. But to me it appears that the principal influence was a commitment to show the nude as an overt expression of sexuality, in opposition to the virtually universal hypocrisy of presenting her as a goddess or some such. The latter allows a conspiracy between artist and viewer that it's all right to look at the nude, because if she is not painted as an image of sexuality then she will not be seen as one. But of course the nude, whether male or female, is always seen to a large degree as a sexual object by half of the population.

There has been a great deal of discussion about the blurring of the distinction between high art and popular culture in modern times, and of when it began. Was it when Andy Warhol gave us Brillo boxes? Or when Duchamp signed a urinal? Or when Braque and

Fort McHenry, East Fort Avenue, 1799 and after, Jean Foncin and others, architects

The site of the successful defense against a British bombardment in 1814 that led to the writing of "The Star-Spangled Banner," our national anthem, Fort McHenry was built from 1799 to 1805. There had been an earlier star-shaped fort built during the Revolutionary War, and the present fort may be in part a carryover of that one. Foncin was the French architect hired in 1799 to oversee the construction of Fort McHenry, named after Marylander James McHenry, who was George Washington's secretary of war. The fort's main feature is the four-sided bastion at each of the five points of the star. The bastions allowed interlocking fields of gunfire in every direction, eliminating blind spots. Later additions to the fort included a V-shaped ravelin in front of the sally port in 1813; a covered passageway enclosing the sally port in 1819, designed by Maximilian Godefroy; and major alterations from 1829 to 1839 that included raising the interior buildings from one to two floors. At that time the fort essentially took on the appearance it has today.

Picasso, the creators of collage, placed bits of everyday objects such as newspapers or tickets in their works? No, it was when Manet raised pornography, the overt representation of the nude as sexual image, to the level of high art. Prostitutes had been represented in high art for a long time, of course, but as objects of ridicule or scorn, not as icons of sex. Sexuality, in *Olympia,* becomes something to worship, as symbolized by the offering of flowers from a devotee that the maid brings to the altar of Olympia's sexuality.

Seeing the painting totally changed my sense of it. From reproductions, I had the idea that the bourgeoisie were wrong to be shocked by *Olympia,* because Manet was showing the prostitute from their point of view, as a brazen hussy. To see the painting is to realize that in it Manet recognizes sexuality as a sacred aspect of life. And so the painting can be seen as the first shot in the sexual revolution, for it is an attempt to liberate sexuality from the realm of conventional morality. The bourgeoisie were absolutely right to be shocked and offended by *Olympia,* for it was they who understood it, not the "enlightened" viewers who discussed it in formal terms.

No work of art has changed before my eyes more than *Olympia* did. It was a revelatory experience.

Thinking about it afterward reminded me of a much earlier example of art changing before one's eyes—certainly less radical or meaningful, but more formative, because it may well have been the birth of this whole aspect of my life with art. At eighteen, between high school and college, on a trip to Europe I took a bus tour to the French chateau country of the Loire valley. We stayed at the town of Tours, and one evening after dinner four or five of us took a stroll and stopped in front of the Cathedral of St.-Gatien, with what a guidebook calls its "twin towers," which were lighted in the evening. They are very much alike, and someone remarked that they were identical. Then someone else said no they weren't and pointed out a tiny difference between them. Then someone else pointed out another, after which we all got into the game of finding differences, and spent about ten minutes standing there and watching those towers change in front of our eyes as a result of looking.

Although I wasn't then conscious of the event's importance, it was probably

my first revelation that art changes, and that it would therefore be something interesting to think about. But why make all this fuss over something like that? Aren't the changes in art that go on in one's mind just enjoyable little musings that make no essential difference to the person who's indulging in them, much less any difference to the art itself? No, in both cases. Thinking about art is both good for the person who does it and good for the art.

Sister Wendy, the English nun who has become an international celebrity for her television programs about art, at one point had a conversation with Bill Moyers in which she says some very pertinent things about the importance of art to one's life. Thinking about art, she says, can make you more able to deal with your own life. She calls this the spiritual power of art, but not in a religious sense.

"The spiritual power is this ability to lift us out of the confines of our ego, out of the traps so many people are in— their relationships, their jobs, their worries (mortgages, health)—and they go round in the cage, and art opens a door and takes you into something bigger than yourself, something immensely exhilarating and refreshing—so when

you come back into your cage you know that's not all there is to life …

"Kenneth Clark used to say that whenever he got deeply depressed he'd go and look at a great work of art. [Here Sister Wendy says the following words are hers, not Clark's.] And there it was, sailing through the centuries, untouched by all our littleness and our anxieties, and we're taken into that, not as an escape, but as a way of coming back into our anxieties better able to put them into perspective. Art is a great means of getting perspective on all that's worrying, depressing, constricting in your life" (Sister Wendy in conversation with Bill Moyers, WGBH Boston video, 1997, minutes 27–28).

That's quite true. But another and possibly even more important reason to think about art for yourself is to exercise the mind. In recent years people have learned a great deal about the importance of physical exercise. It can earn you a more attractive body, prolong your life, and make you feel better all the way through life. It seems that less attention is paid to mental exercise, which is just as important and in much the same ways. It can earn you a more attractive mind (in conversation, in writing, in every way), it can quite possibly prolong the life of the mind, and it can make you feel mentally better all the way through life.

Sister Wendy speaks to this, when asked what art has done for her: "I hope it's made me a more sensitive and more alert person. The one fatal thing is to be a zombie, and I think we're all in danger of living part of our lives at zombie level. But I think art helps one to be perpetually there, as it were . . . alert, constant, in the moment" (minutes 22–23).

Art is more important for that purpose than ever before, because since the advent of television we have all become more zombiesque than when we engaged to a greater extent in conversation, reading, and playing games. But modern art, and the way it has been received, have perversely removed it more from personal response at the moment in history when it needed most to encourage personal response. Sister Wendy refers to that, too, when Moyers asks, "Do you think that most of us are born with the potential to respond to art as you hope we will?"

"I'm sure everyone has this capacity," she replies, but goes on to say that all too often, "it's not activated." She blames that in part on art critics, "who speak in a kind of high-falutin' way." That gives people the wrong idea about responding to art, she thinks. It tells people "that unless you're highly educated and very bright and know the right language you really haven't got any right to have an opinion" (minute 16).

That's not entirely the fault of the critics. In the modern age, as art became more abstract, the more scholarly critics naturally addressed it in more abstract and theoretical ways. But the popular critic, such as the newspaper critic, has an obligation to try and make art accessible to the art-going public. In doing that, we're trying to help people to think for themselves, not to do thinking for them. But all too often the public thinks of our thoughts not as a tool to aid them in construction of their thoughts, but as a construction that saves them the work.

The age of modern art contains a paradox. In recent decades, more and more people have gone to see art, primarily in museums, often called the cathedrals of the present age. But paradoxically, many people feel that they haven't got sufficient knowledge to understand modern art, so they don't try. They go to the museum carrying with them an invisible wall of perceived intellectual inferiority, and hold it up between them and the works of art. I saw a classic example of that when attending a 1984 retrospective of the works of Willem de Kooning at the Whitney Museum of American Art in New York.

Now de Kooning has certainly been the subject of a good deal of esoteric, theory-based criticism. But in my opinion, while it may not be easy to understand him completely, it is not difficult to respond to him. His work possesses emotion, aggressiveness, even violence, and also a great deal of beauty in terms of color and the dynamics of brushstroke. No theoretical background is necessary to get all that out of it. What people tend not to understand about modern art is that whatever theoretical background gets attached to it by critics, it was made by people who have the same emotions, hopes, fears, desires, and need to communicate that people have always had. Art is humanity (the artist) speaking to humanity (the viewer), just as it has always been, and the two don't need to connect through some theoretical labyrinth any more than they ever did.

While at the de Kooning exhibit, I caught sight of a couple looking utterly blank and bewildered. They obviously thought they couldn't relate to the work at all, so they weren't trying. Just then a docent began a gallery talk, and the husband said, "Maybe she can tell us what this stuff is all about." Well, she couldn't.

I'm all for docents, and think they do a fine job. And I'm sure the Whitney docent did a fine job. But what a work of art is "all about" is how it relates to you, how it makes your mind work, and by coming into contact with it only through someone else's mind you're not really relating to it. If the docent or the curator gives you something that helps you then relate to it for yourself, that's fine. But I had the sense that that couple was going to listen to what the docent said, think they had done what they came to do, and go away. That is not the way to relate to art.

The way to relate to art is to think about it and find out how it relates to you. That will have an immensely beneficial effect on your mind. And that in turn will have an immensely beneficial effect on art.

Only when we think about art does it become important to our lives. And only when we recognize that importance are we likely to make some kind of contribution toward it—whether we buy art, write about it, work for or contribute to an art institution, vote for those who also believe in its importance, or however each of us chooses to contribute. When enough people contribute, art gains in importance, gets more funds, and so on. It's a circle, and the circle grows larger or smaller, depending on how many people think art is important to their lives. The essential element of the health of art is that people think about art.

Art changes. We change. Both change for the better when we think about art, for the worse when we don't.

When one thinks of a classical façade, particularly of domestic scale, one thinks symmetrical and often based on the number 5. It can be either five-bay town house—for example, Federal period Carroll Mansion (ca. 1812) and Classical Revival period Mount Vernon Club (1842) and Hackerman House (1850)—or five-part country house—for example, Federal period Homewood (1801–4) and Georgian/colonial Mount Clare (1753–87 and after), the last as presently constituted. The five-part façade seems to be especially appealing because it's restful to the eye. It has more amplitude than a three-part façade but its number is instantly recognizable and doesn't have to be counted up, as a seven- or nine-part façade does. As illustrated by the distinguished examples above, some of the leading classical façades of any community will be five-part.

Because, however, the primary subject matter of this book's photographs is aspects of architecture rather than façades, there is no photograph herein showing a five-part classical façade. So to satisfy to some degree the human eye's apparent hunger for five-part symmetry, we include this curiosity. It has the appearance of nothing so much as

134

an upstart mocking two kinds of what might be called "establishment" architecture, in a mode reminiscent of how, in Marx Brothers movies, Groucho used to mock the very proper ladies played by Margaret Dumont.

Behind the obviously twentieth-century and probably industrial façade is a building that looks like it was a house which, whatever its age, conformed to a gabled, dormered, bay-windowed, asymmetrical, Victorian-flavor "picturesque" house. "I'll ridicule that style," the upstart said. So he put on aluminum siding, covered up most if not all of the windows, and added a façade that made what can be seen of the older house look antiquated, ugly, and out of place. And "I'll ridicule the classical façade at the same time," the upstart said. So instead of a façade with a columned portico in the center flanked by two windows on each side, he centered the whole thing on a glass brick window, an art deco commercial element that became a cliché (see the Senator Theater), flanked by two doors, each of which makes the other look redundant, in turn flanked by two blind windows. The whole thing makes something ridiculous out of the five-part classical façade. In effect this says to classical

architects, "You think your five-part façade is inherently beautiful, do you? Well, just look at this and say it's beautiful."

But the upstart actually defeats himself. Any book that has anything to do with the beauty of architecture ought to include a picture like this in celebration of fine architects. This says it's not the design element, it's the architect who creates beauty, as this mishmash makes clear.

600 block West University Parkway

This photograph of part of an empty room recalls Walker Evans's 1930s photographs of buildings associated with working-class America.

It's probably easier to notice the differences, but the similarities run deeper. One Evans photograph in particular, a 1935 image of Bethlehem, Pennsylvania, offers especially interesting comparisons (though others would do just as well). It's cluttered looking at first glance—cemetery in the foreground, row of modest workers' houses in the middle ground, industrial buildings in the background—and it seems to have a deliberately haphazard composition.

The photograph shown here exhibits several obvious differences—an interior versus exterior shot, an empty rather than filled-up look, a spare and manifestly quite calculated composition. But even in strictly visual terms there are more important similarities. In both pictures, things are cut off, giving a sense of continuance beyond the picture frame. The compositions are creatively asymmetrical, generating a satisfying sense of tension. And a single object—in the Evans a stone cross, in this photograph the radiator—serves as the focus around which the rest of the picture arranges itself.

The symbolic similarities are even more important. In both pictures there is no human figure, and that makes the human presence all the more resonant. These works are about lives lived, and more to the point they are about people whose lives will not be immortal but who count. The houses we see, from the outside and the inside, are not grand; they speak of the values of domesticity, of family, of everyday life. The Evans picture tells us more specifically about that life—how it is bounded by the factory and the graveyard—but both it and the photograph shown here let us know that what we don't see is more essential than what we do, in two senses. The people we don't see are the real subjects of these works, not the buildings we do see. And intangibles, not tangibles, are the essence of life.

St. Mary's Seminary Chapel, 600 North Paca Street, 1808, Maximilian Godefroy, architect

While it is considerably less than Godefroy designed, this little chapel building has characteristics of Gothic architecture, including pointed arches, groined vaults, stained-glass windows, and a substitute for what would have been a rose window above the main door. The interior has rows of columns with acanthus-leaf capitals. Several changes have taken place over the years, including one by Cochran, Stephenson, and Donkervoet in 1968, which lightened the interior and returned it as much as possible to Godefroy's design.

The term *downsizing* was invented, probably by someone in public relations, as a euphemism for layoffs, which had earlier been invented as a euphemism for firing people. But at St. Mary's Seminary Chapel, built almost two centuries before *downsizing* came into the language, the word applies in the literal sense, as this photograph of one of Baltimore's most curious buildings indicates.

A little history's in order. St. Mary's Seminary, now occupying a generous building and property on Roland Avenue in North Baltimore, was established by the Sulpician Order in 1791. Fourteen years later, Maximilian Godefroy (see also p. 63), in exile from France for his opposition to Napoleon, came to America and settled in Baltimore to teach architecture, among other things, at St. Mary's College, also run by the Sulpicians. His first building in Baltimore was this little chapel, designed in 1806, built by 1808, and still standing off of the 600 block of Paca Street, where St. Mary's originated.

Godefroy became a friend of Benjamin Henry Latrobe, who was working on the Catholic Cathedral (now Basilica of the Assumption) in Baltimore. Latrobe in 1805 had submitted two designs for the cathedral, one Gothic and the other Classical, the latter being chosen. Whether Godefroy saw Latrobe's Gothic design before he submitted his design for this building isn't a matter of record, but it's not unlikely that he did. At any rate, because Latrobe's Gothic design was not chosen, Godefroy's chapel became the first Gothic religious building in Baltimore and one of the first Gothic buildings in the country.

Originally the chapel interior was to reach to the top of the front wall, the end of which can be seen here rising above the first-floor cornice as merely a façade. There was to be a row of stained-glass windows giving onto the interior and centered on a rose window, and the whole was to be topped by a tower, a much more appealing look as seen in Godefroy's original design. And the façade was to be faced with stone.

Because of financial constraints, a lot of that was eliminated. The original tower never got built, and the stone façade became more lowly brick. The interior (plaster) vaulting was lowered, bringing down the roof level and leaving the upper part of the front façade as a wall with nothing behind it. (Why it wasn't simply eliminated, also in the name of economy, is anybody's guess.)

My guess says that it was left to appease Godefroy, a contentious character.) The row of stained-glass windows became niches, which were supposed to hold statues of the twelve apostles, but they were never added. The two lower niches flanking the front door Godefroy designed as stained-glass windows also, but that never got done.

The photograph shows the church to have one feature of Gothic architecture that it wouldn't have had if built as originally designed. Had the side walls extended to the height of the front wall, they would have eliminated the flying buttresses supporting the front wall on either end, one of which shows in the photograph. So in that way the chapel is more Gothic than Godefroy's design.

Resurgam Gallery, 910 South Charles Street

Juxtaposition can make a lot of difference.

That electrical mess in the corner would not look sightly under any conditions. But the nearby curtain tied into a knot makes the electrical mess more of an interesting comparison than just some ugly wiring. One notices how the lines of both flow downward, and how the light shining on the hard round switch boxes compares with the light that bathes the curtain's similarly shaped knot. One wonders, did the person who tied the curtain in a knot do so in preparation for a trip, to keep the bottom of the curtain from gathering dust resting on a horizontal surface? Or was it to make people notice the comparison? Or was it to make the wiring "more comfortable," and bring to mind similar acts of courtesy?

We've all heard such stories—the one about the man who came to a formal affair in tennis shoes, so his host excused himself and came back also wearing tennis shoes—and we've wondered whether to believe them. I was witness to just such an act, performed by the most exquisitely courteous person I have ever known. I will call her Henrietta because that's not her name. A long time ago, maybe twenty years

or so, Henrietta had a visitor from out of town, a dear person who is also a friend and whom I will call Sally. One night the two of them, plus Henrietta's husband and a few other people, came to our house for dinner. During dinner, Sally told a story about an acquaintance, which required her to quote the acquaintance uttering the most extreme four-letter word in the language. The group wasn't prudish, but there might have been a tiny lull in the conversation, embarrassing to Sally. Henrietta, sensing with lightning speed that that might happen, instantly and seamlessly launched a story of her own, in which she, too, no later than the second sentence, uttered the same four-letter word, the only time I have ever heard her use it, and by doing so made everyone comfortable with Sally's having used it.

Later I reflected that had I been as supremely kind and courteous as Henrietta, I might have done the thing myself, and it would have been even more appropriate coming from the host. I didn't think of it, but I'll never forget it, and this picture seems like nothing so much as an illustration of that beautiful act.

If God is in the details, He was looking over the shoulder of the architect who drew this one. It is not a great detail, but think of it in terms of where it is. It is a minor side entrance of the Rotunda on 40th Street between Keswick Road and Roland Avenue. It's not seen from the front or back of the building, and such entrances often have basic architectural detailing if any at all.

Consider, then, the success of this modest architectural detail. The section of the lower floor that we see is faced with stonework, of no structural function and therefore purely decorative. A pentagonal, pediment-like piece of stone rests on the course just over the doorway, giving it more visual importance than it would otherwise have. The stonework around the doorway has raised edges framing an indented center, adding a touch of formality and prominence. The projecting stone sills of the two windows give them just the right touch of emphasis. And it's impossible to imagine how the windows' proportions and placement in the wall could be better related to the doorway.

Some thought went into the achievement of this architectural grace note, and the photographer emphasizes its felicity by placing the camera at a slight angle, thus achieving a vitality of image that would not be there if the thing had been taken straight on.

Next page:

Rotunda, 40th Street between Roland Avenue and Keswick Road, 1921, Otto G. Simonson, architect

Built for the Maryland Casualty Company, this H-shaped building has been described as Georgian in style. That's a confusing but here not inappropriate designation. As English architecture, Georgian covers the four kings named George, from 1714 to 1830, and sometimes Queen Anne (1702–14) is thrown in as well. In American terms, it's usually used to designate colonial architecture based on English models, especially those baroque in flavor. The Rotunda, something of an odd pastiche, may fit most comfortably under such a vague term. Its main façade has a massive and rather dead classical portico under a more baroque Christopher Wren–inspired tower of several sections rising to a dome and cupola. The building's architectural decorations, including swags, scrolls, and rosettes, have an Adamesque flavor far too delicate for its lumpish overall proportions. When Maryland Casualty moved to a new headquarters next door, the building was renovated with awkward infills on both sides and opened in 1971 as a shopping and office complex called the Rotunda. It is still a shopping and office complex, and is still called the Rotunda.

The previous entry had the distinction of being a pleasing detail on a less than great work of architecture. An attractive passage of brushwork, let us say, on the canvas of an American Impressionist, that would equally stand out as not up to par on a canvas by Pissarro.

Context matters. If that doorway were on this building it would be an eyesore. Because here we have one of Baltimore's finest buildings by one of the best architects who ever worked here: the Baltimore Museum of Art's original 1920s building by John Russell Pope, the greatest American Classical Revival architect of the twentieth century. As Latrobe in the first half of the nineteenth century gave Baltimore its greatest building and one of its loveliest little buildings, both in the Classical style and the latter on the grounds of this museum, so Pope in the first half of the twentieth century gave Baltimore some of its finest buildings of the period.

He did considerable work here, beginning in 1905 with his addition of the eastern third of the Garrett Jacobs Mansion on Mount Vernon Place, the western two-thirds of which had been designed by Stanford White two decades

earlier. Next, in 1914, he designed the James Swan Frick House in Guilford, not the largest but the most impressive mansion in Baltimore. It is in the Adamesque style, named after the eighteenth-century British architects Robert and James Adam (see p. 154), and is one of four houses in the Adamesque style that Pope designed between 1912 and 1916, from Washington to Long Island.

Pope is also the architect of the University Baptist Church at 3501 North Charles Street and of the Scottish Rite Temple of Freemasonry at Charles and 39th streets. The Baltimore Museum of Art building, opened in 1929, is Pope's Baltimore masterpiece.

During the 1930s Pope designed four other art museum buildings, the Duveen Gallery for Parthenon Sculptures at the British Museum and the modern sculpture wing at the Tate Gallery, both in London, the Frick Collection in New York, and the National Gallery in Washington, all to some degree based on the Baltimore Museum of Art, Pope's first art museum design. As Pope's biographer Steven McLeod Bedford has written, "The Baltimore Museum of Art set the standard for

Baltimore Museum of Art, 10 Art Museum Drive near Charles and 31st streets, 1926–29, John Russell Pope, architect; 1934–37, John Russell Pope, architect; 1950s, Wrenn, Lewis, and Jencks, architects; 1982 and 1994, Bower, Lewis, Thrower, architects; 1988, Sasaki Associates, architects

Of the current sprawling complex, Pope designed the original building, with a façade centered on a portico flanked by niches, and columned openings facing east and west on the two ends. The interior consists of a grand columned central hall flanked by galleries. In 1935 Pope added a courtyard behind the original building, which as planned has acted as the core of the entire complex and the center of the east-west axial plan along which subsequent parts have been added. Immediately around the court, forming parts of what from the inside seem like one central building, are the Jacobs Wing to the east, added by Pope in 1937, and the May Wing (to the north), Cone Wing (to the west), and the Woodward Wing (to the northwest), all by Wrenn, Lewis, and Jencks in the 1950s.

Later additions, quite obviously distinct from the original structure, are the east wing of 1982 by Bower, Lewis, Thrower of Philadelphia, the 1988 Levi Sculpture Garden by Sasaki Associates of Boston, and the 1994 west wing called the West Wing for Contemporary Art and also by Bower, Lewis, Thrower. Fortunately, one cannot see the whole complex from end to end from any earthbound point of view, and Pope's central façade still leaves the major impression. Relative to the Baltimore Museum of Art, see also the next entry, plus pages 42 (vine on wall), 74 (empty niche), and 4 (Oakland Spring House).

Pope's future museum designs" (*John Russell Pope, Architect of Empire,* 1998, p. 170).

Dealing with the exterior, of which this photograph pictures a detail, Bedford writes, the "reserved monumentality of the exterior is relieved by the carefully placed string-courses, niches, and recessed panels. The limestone masonry is graded in size and tone to create an image of strength and continuous tonality" (p. 170).

If God is in the details, here it's in a different sense from the previous entry. There, it's that one detail looks better than one might have expected from its minor location with respect to the building. Here, it's that no detail was slighted. Every part of the building is beautifully done, in terms of proportions, materials, and aspects of design down to the tiniest. Here we have no entryway or part of the principal façade, but a little cul-de-sac on the east side of the building with basement windows. The handsome, varied, and perfectly laid stonework, the unnecessary but for that reason especially pleasing posts that give elegant entry to this small space, the beautifully shaped and proportioned windows with just the right amount of wall space above them up to

the course that pulls everything together visually and the ledge above it—all testify to Pope's classical academic training in combination with a highly refined aesthetic sense.

One wouldn't have to be aware of the building as a whole to know that a superior architect worked here.

Baltimore Museum of Art, Art Museum Drive near Charles and 31st streets. For architectural description, see the previous entry.

While we're on the subject of the Baltimore Museum of Art, here's one more photograph that shows a part of it. To the left a part of the Jacobs wing, where again we see Pope's great care down to every detail. To the right, a wing added in 1982 that is obviously not part of the main complex when the front façade of the wing is viewed as a whole. Designed by Bower, Lewis, Thrower of Philadelphia, the 1982 wing's modern first-floor entrance, surmounted by a second-floor wall of glass ending at a gray-tiled serpentine wall on the exterior of the auditorium, all pronounce the wing a distinctly separate building.

Yet the architects also managed to pay their respects to Pope, as seen here. The small part of wall to the right of the picture, with a black railing at the top, is the left end of the 1982 wing's first-floor entrance façade. It's done in stonework to match Pope's, and it balances at every level. The length of the initial block of each row of stonework, going up the wall from the bottom of the picture, mirrors the corresponding block on the Pope wall. Proceeding upward, there are two narrower rows of stone facing topped by a wider row, also mir-

roring the Pope wall. Finally, the band at the top, plus the height of the railing, visually complement the next stone row up in the Pope building.

The Bower, Lewis, Thrower wing was controversial when it opened. Some architecture critics derided it, while others defended it. As a whole, the 1982 wing's façade looks radically different from the museum to which it's connected. This picture, however, selects just the right corner of the façade to show the architects' homage to Pope, which most people who see the wing as a whole probably don't notice. In other words, When the Part Serves Better than the Whole: Part IV.

Roland Park Public School, 5200 block Roland Avenue, 1925, Edward L. Palmer Jr., architect; addition, 1930, Palmer and Lamdin, architects

This large institutional building has touches of the Italian Romanesque, especially in the one stylistic emphasis, a tower with rows of rounded arches: four arches at the top of vertical openings separated by columns with Ionic-like capitals and a row of eight blind arches below the openings. Plus blind arches above windows on several façades, and small octagonal windows giving variety here and there.

Why does this picture, which I know to be of a place in Baltimore, speak to me of the South, and what does that say about my biases?

The cracked pavement, the ailanthus trees (commonly called trash trees) in various stages of growth, the crude and somewhat disintegrating concrete wall surface, the louvered windows and pull-down metal door, the long shadows and the bright sunshine that suggest a dying hot summer day, the chain link fence at the top, the apparent pile of trash by the wall at right—all add up to an implication of degeneracy.

So why should a picture that suggests degeneracy bring thoughts of the South to mind? It's part of American culture to view the South that way. So many writers, creative and otherwise, southern and otherwise, have depicted it in that fashion. Probably the three greatest creative writers with works placed in the South are Mark Twain, William Faulkner, and Tennessee Williams. Williams's best-drawn characters, Amanda and Blanche, stand as symbols of the South's descent. Faulkner's novels portray a land of deterioration. And Twain's Huckleberry Finn helps African American Jim flee

from the cruelties of a slaveholding society.

H. L. Mencken, in his highly controversial 1920 essay on the South called "The Sahara of the Bozart," terms the region a "vast … vacuity," a "stupendous region of worn-out farms, shoddy cities and paralyzed cerebrums," and "almost as sterile, artistically, intellectually, culturally, as the Sahara Desert." But he credits it as having had at one time—that is, before the Civil War— "a civilization of manifold excellences … undoubtedly the best that These States have ever seen" (*H. L. Mencken: The American Scene,* 1965, pp. 157–58).

But Mencken was not born until fifteen years after the Civil War and had no firsthand knowledge of the antebellum South. A person who did have such knowledge was Frederick Law Olmsted, who in 1853, before he became America's first and preeminent landscape architect, progressed through the South from Virginia to Texas to experience its civilization and report on it for the *New York Daily Times.* He found it wanting in comparison with the North, not only in terms of its dependence on slavery, but in every regard from transportation to literacy. "Olmsted's South bore little resemblance to the mythic Old South

of elegant mansions and graceful cotillion balls," writes Olmsted's biographer Witold Rybczynski. "Although he saw some beautiful plantation houses, he found civic society in towns to be woefully undeveloped. Although this part of the United States had been settled as long as—or, in some cases, longer than—the Northern states, he was shocked to find that it was a different, backward country. Beyond Virginia, he wrote, there were few libraries, colleges, or concert halls. Local book and newspaper publishers were rare. That was hardly surprising. Literacy—among whites—was considerably lower than in the North" (*A Clearing in the Distance,* 1999, p. 119).

But if the South has been commonly characterized as more degenerate than the North, that makes it immensely more interesting than the North. Vices are always more interesting than virtues, and the same is of course true of immorality versus morality, degeneracy versus rectitude, and all the other ways of putting it. If the South was indeed more degenerate than the North for a period of its history, that is no doubt much less if at all true today, which only makes the South much less interesting today. If you question that, let me put to you this question as an answer. If you had to choose between two plays to go to, and the only thing you knew about the plays was that one had a neat, clean, fussy-looking patio as a set, and the other had this picture as a set, which would you choose?

    Q.E.D.

When architects Pell and Corbett designed their 1908 building as the new home of the Maryland Institute College of Art (whose downtown building had burned in the 1904 Baltimore Fire), they created it in the then-popular Renaissance style, specifically giving the exterior an Italian Renaissance palazzo form. The white marble facing on the exterior walls may bring Venice to mind, but the building's massing and fenestration closely resemble those of Florentine palazzi, especially Palazzo Medici-Riccardi and Palazzo Strozzi.

Renaissance, of course, refers to rebirth of interest in classical antiquity, and the interior great hall of the building contains architectural and other references to classicism resurrected in the Renaissance, combined with copies of ancient sculpture. This photograph captures the complexity of reference that makes the room well worth a visit.

Take the columns, for example. All three major orders of Western civilization columns—Doric, Ionic, and Corinthian—originated in Greece; but columns supporting arches speak of Rome, for the Romans created the arch and the dome. These columns' references are considerably more complicated than that. In the Renaissance

there were composite columns combin-
ing the rams' horn spirals of the Ionic
capital with the foliate carving of the
Corinthian capital. These capitals are
in general such a composite. But this
specific design, with regimented rows
of single leaves standing at attention,
not overlapping, and with a dog-eared
curve at the top, directly descends from
the ca. 1770 design by English architects Robert and James Adam for the
Society of Arts building that was part
of their Adelphi complex in London.
The Adam brothers created a classical
style known as Adamesque, to some
extent based upon eighteenth-century
archaeological discoveries at Hercula-
neum and Pompeii, freely adapted by
the brothers.

So these column capitals have double lineages from the Renaissance—
composite capitals in general and specific Adamesque design—plus double
lineages from the ancient world—Ionic
order from Greece and Adamesque design based in part on Roman archaeological discoveries.

Another classical descent with an
English connection exists in the copy
of the Greek sculpture of the river god
Ilissus (ca. 450–430 B.C.). The original
comes from the western pediment of

the Parthenon, but shortly after 1800
it was moved to England as one of the
Elgin Marbles housed for the last two
centuries at the British Museum. The
sculpture partly seen in the shadowy
background, of Hermes and Diony-
sus (ca. 340 B.C.), also copies a Greek
original, but in this case the original
remains in Greece, at the Archaeological Museum at Olympia.

The room contains numerous other
references, not seen here, to the Renaissance and the ancient world. Go see for
yourself. In the daytime, in my experience, you can just walk into the building and take a good look at the hall.
Finally, it's a nice touch that we can see
a mosaic floor design, for the Romans
were famous for their mosaics, and this
one provides one more classical connection.

Caroline Street south of Eastern Avenue

Here we have an indictment of much of the worst that America has to offer. Reading from back to front, what's happened to the gable at right rear is hard to tell, but it seems to have lost much of its brick facing and shows the patchwork way it was either put together originally or has been repaired. That has a lot to say about American cities, and the treatment of them. In America cities do not get the resources they need because they are thought of as homes of poverty and crime, and not given credit as homes of the arts, sciences, and learning that make a civilization flourish.

The gimcrack Statue of Liberty rip-off, presumably raising her light bulb to draw the attention of the passerby to the Tutti Frutti Ice Cream Co., is an example of one of commercialism's worst aspects, its willingness to debase even the revered symbol of our highest values to make a buck.

And the concrete veneer facing on the building, presumably Formstone, is a kind of aesthetic horror, to my knowledge unique to Baltimore. But in a larger sense it's merely a local case of what Mencken in a 1927 essay called "The Libido for the Ugly" that he thought endemic to America. "Here," he wrote, "is

something that the psychologists have so far neglected: the love of ugliness for its own sake, the lust to make the world intolerable. Its habitat is the United States" (*The Vintage Mencken,* 1955, p. 181).

Physically and metaphysically this is a vast nation, encompassing everything from the sublime to the execrable. A good bit of the latter is either shown or implied here.

Hydraulic Service building, Barclay Street, north of University Parkway and 33rd Street

The expression "this building was made for its site" usually has a double meaning: it enhances its site from a distance, and it is placed to take advantage of the best views the site has to offer. This structure fits neither of those meanings. The hydraulic service building was not made to enhance its site, on Barclay Street just off of 33rd Street and University Parkway. And it was not made to take advantage of views because there are no extraordinary views to take advantage of. Yet it was probably "made for its site" more literally than any other building to which the expression has been attached.

The building sits in a triangle defined by Barclay Street and two alleys, one of which runs perpendicular to Barclay on the far side of the building as we look at it. The other alley, on the left side of the picture, runs diagonal to Barclay Street and connects up with the other alley at a distance shortly beyond the end of the left wall of the building. From our point of view, the building looks like a trapezoid, with one back wall connecting the two long ones in the photograph. But it is actually a pentagon. We can see three walls, and there are two walls that we can't see.

This building isn't aesthetically pleasing, nor was it meant to be. But it may be unique in terms of outline and dimensions, and it was most definitely made for its site.

Hackerman House carriage house, Walters Art Museum, South Washington Place, 600 block North Charles Street

For the architectural description of Hackerman House, see page 56. The domed structure above the carriage house is part of the link between the museum's 1904 building and Hackerman House, added 1989–91 by James R. Grieves Associates, architects of the Hackerman House renovation/restoration.

Shadows can aid or obstruct vision (speaking visually here, not symbolically). In this photograph they do both, but above all they add interest. In fact, the picture's about shadows.

The architecture shown consists of two small parts of the Walters Art Museum's complex that borders the entire western side of South Washington Place, between Centre and Monument streets. Here we have the alley that parallels those two streets halfway up the block. The lower, one-story building that supports the upper structure is the carriage house behind Hackerman House, One West Mount Vernon Place, one of the finest town houses of the nineteenth century, now the Walters Museum of Asian Art. The upper structure is the bridge over the alley from the Walters main building to Hackerman House, plus a kind of lobby (the bay-windowed and domed part) from which one descends by elevator or stairs to lower-level galleries connecting to the Hackerman House main building.

The carriage house architecture is pretty elaborate for its function, with round, demilune, and rectangular windows, an arched doorway for pedestrians and a garage-type door farther back for carriages or automobiles, a belt course halfway up the wall on the two visible sides, and a prominent, crisp cornice where the bright sunlight creates shadows that emphasize the dentil decorations on the side facing us and obscure them along the alley side. The shadows in alley doors and windows also give them depth and emphasis, and the broader diagonal shadows covering parts of the back wall add drama.

Above, one at first wonders what the black rectangle in the bridge wall is—maybe a hole?—for it appears too long for a shadow defining what looks like a shallow indentation of the wall. But on closer examination it turns out to be a shadow, and the indentation turns out to be deeper than it looks initially. Without the shadow, one probably wouldn't notice that detail of the architecture.

The picture gains charm it would not otherwise possess from another shadow, that of the top of a street lamp with street sign, which travels across the sidewalk and up the carriage house wall. It's eye-catching, and no doubt caught the eye of the photographer. Some photographs look carefully planned, others spur-of-the-moment. It's obvious to which group this one belongs.

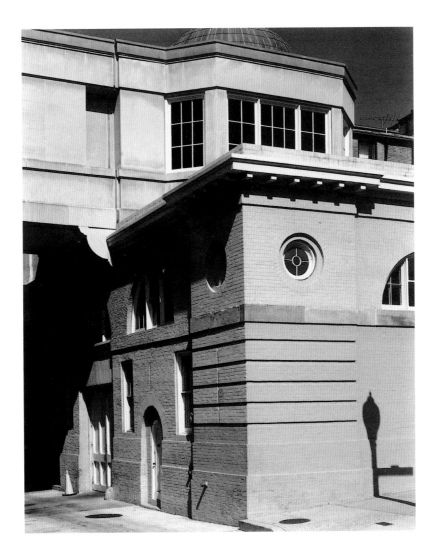

Mount Clare Museum House, Carroll Park, southwest Baltimore, 1753–87, with later alterations, architect unknown

This is the only surviving colonial plantation house in Baltimore City. Charles Carroll, Barrister, tore down an earlier house and between 1757 and 1760 built partly upon its foundations the main block, with two-story pilasters on the garden front, plus a washhouse and an orangery on either end of the complex, as separate buildings. In 1766 a new front was added, with a Palladian-windowed chamber above a pillared entry, plus office and kitchen wings at either end, connected to the house by hyphens, plus two smaller buildings between the major complex and the washhouse and orangery. In 1787, the barrister's widow added a greenhouse and service building at either end, extending the complex to its greatest length. Of the present complex the main block is original; the hyphens and wings by Wyatt and Nolting date from 1907.

This picture of a detail of Mount Clare Museum House in southwest Baltimore, including about half of the portico and the front door, reminds me of my late friend Michael F. Trostel, the well-known restoration architect. His distinguished career included projects such as Davidge Hall at the University of Maryland Baltimore Campus, the Robert Long House in Fells Point, Long Hill in Wicomico County, Mount Airy in Prince George's County, and Mount Clare. Mike worked at Mount Clare not only as an architect—he also wrote a book about its history, *Mount Clare,* published in 1981.

Charles Carroll, Barrister, built Mount Clare in a Georgian colonial style in several stages beginning in the 1750s. He ordered the stone columns of the portico from England, and they were shipped in sections, as indicated by the cracks seen here in the stucco facing. Four years after the barrister's death in 1783, his widow, Margaret Tilghman Carroll, made slight changes to the main house—a window, a mantelpiece, and so on. Mike wrote of the changes that they "are more in the Federal style of which Baltimore was a leader than in the Georgian style of An-

napolis, indicating that as early as 1787 Baltimore was supplanting Annapolis as the leader of style" (*A Guide to Baltimore Architecture,* 1997, p. 235).

Mrs. Carroll also added outbuildings to make the complex eleven parts and 360 feet long, its greatest extent. Over the years all but the main building, shown here, disappeared, but new hyphens and wings were added in 1907, designed by architects Wyatt and Nolting.

That was the extent of it when Mike went to work there in the 1970s. He was the right person, for he was that rare individual, someone of strongly held opinions but at the same time professionally pragmatic rather than dogmatic. He would tell you in no uncertain terms what he thought of everything from architecture to other people, and when he had an opinion he seldom changed it. He once remarked that any novel was like any other novel, just a story, indicating that to him novels had no aesthetic qualities. When I replied that it would make as much sense if I said all architecture was alike, that a garage and Blenheim Palace were simply the enclosure of space for a utilitarian purpose, he of course said such a state-

ment would be nonsense. But it didn't in the least alter his low opinion of the novel as an art form.

When it came to his work on architecture, on the other hand, he was flexible. One can imagine a person of such strong opinions might recommend tearing down the replacement hyphens and wings, and perhaps even removing Mrs. Carroll's Federal alterations to the main house, to return what was left of the original structure to pure Georgian style. But no, he did everything he could for what was there. That was in line with his general philosophy that a restoration architect shouldn't insist on absolute purity of style or period, but decide what period it was best to take the building back to, and then do the best one could with that.

He took a similar approach to the restoration of Homewood in the late 1980s. He had wanted the job himself, but it was given to a New York firm. He was put on an advisory committee. When the New York firm wanted to paint the interior in the bright colors that were historically probably the second color scheme, rather than the first off-white color scheme, he might have objected that they were being inauthentic to the original appearance of the house and oughtn't to be allowed to do that. But he didn't. He generously expressed the opinion that the house would look much better and make a better tourist attraction with the bright colors, so they should do it. They did, and Homewood looks great.

He was also willing to play the point man. He once designed a new house for a man whom he described as the most demanding and disagreeable client he ever had. The client unceasingly complained about the contractors as the building was going on, always finding fault. But Mike kept the client and the contractors apart, and played the role of go-between and diplomat. As a result, the job got done, the contractors didn't quit or get fired, and the client was satisfied at the end.

Mike was also generous. When we moved into our first house back in 1976, he suggested several changes to give us the optimum living conditions—removal of a closet to enlarge a room, addition of double doors, and so on. The house also needed much other work from floors redone to wiring, painting, and the like. For a period of about two months Mike stopped by every single working day to check on what was being done—not only his work, but the electrical work, floor refinishing, and so on—and to show the workmen that he was keeping a close eye on them. At the end, his total fee was $550. That was a good while ago, but even back then it was a ridiculously low amount.

Mount Clare was Mike Trostel's favorite job, and whenever I see it I remember him.

Poured concrete as a structural building material had a brief life during the development of Roland Park in the first decade of the twentieth century. In 1905 it was used for a group of five connected houses in the 800 block of West University Parkway, designed by Edward L. Palmer Jr. in a somewhat Arts and Crafts style.

Much later, toward the end of the century, Baltimore modern architect Alexander Cochran said that the same use of concrete was not to occur again in Baltimore until the 1960s, when it was used for the Mechanic theater downtown. In essence he was right, that after this brief period it was not used again until the 1960s, but technically he was wrong, for the two other prominent uses of poured concrete in Roland Park were just after the Palmer houses.

One was the University Parkway bridge of 1908 (see next entry). It is just outside the boundaries of Roland Park, but the creation of University Parkway connecting Roland Park with the north-south arteries Charles, St. Paul, and Calvert streets, was brought about by Edward Bouton, president of the Roland Park Company.

The most prominent use of poured concrete was between the dates of

*St. David's Church, 4700 Roland
Avenue at Oakdale Road,
1906–7, Ellicott and Emmart,
architects*

In terms of architectural history, the church's form shares Renaissance (broadly speaking) and early Christian influences, as opposed to medieval (Romanesque or Gothic). As pointed out by Travers Nelson, the façade, with its side doors flanking a main section centered on a window in a stepped-back arch with pediment above and doorway (or in this case recessed and pedimented plaque) below, resembles German baroque churches of the seventeenth and eighteenth centuries. Examples include St. Michael at Berg-am-Leim, Saint Nicholas at Prague, and the Frauenkirche at Dresden. The higher main section and lower side doors indicate the interior basilica form: nave separated from side aisles by a series of four arches on each side, clerestory windows above, all leading to the semicircular apse with a quarter-sphere upper section painted to resemble the sky. The interior has some resemblance to sixth-century churches in Ravenna such as San Apollinare in Classe (534–539) and San Francesco (560).

those two structures, in the 1906–7 construction of St. David's Episcopal Church at Roland Avenue and Oakdale Road, on land also given for the purpose by the Roland Park Company under Bouton's direction.

The architects of the church were Ellicott and Emmart, a prominent firm of the time who did much work in Roland Park, where Ellicott also lived. They designed St. David's in the Renaissance style, and this view of the apse end of the church from Oakdale Road, with an octagonal library in the foreground, shows poured concrete as a happy choice of building material.

There were several choices for churches. One was rough-cut stone, but that is more appropriate for Gothic buildings, the style of two other churches within a block of St. David's. A Renaissance building might have had a brick structure faced with marble or limestone, as the Renaissance main building of the Maryland Institute College of Art of the same period (1908). But that would surely have been much more expensive. Or it could have been of brick either painted to look like stone, brick faced with stucco, or brick left bare. But the last would not have looked as appropriate to a Renaissance building as it does to a Colonial Revival

building. And with brick painted to look like stone or covered with stucco, there probably would not have been the ability to produce such well-proportioned details as the molding process of poured concrete can produce. Note here the crisp, stone-like pilasters and quoins around the apse and at the angles of the octagon. They give the church a fine, formal appearance that it likely could not have had with any other building material except an expensive stone facing.

Poured concrete proved a successful use of building material in the Roland Park examples, and it was a mystery to me why, after the quite brief period of about 1905–10, it was abandoned in Baltimore until the 1960s. Later I talked to Baltimore architect Travers Nelson, who explained that after the Baltimore Fire of 1904, poured concrete had brief popularity in Baltimore because it was thought a particularly effective fireproof method of building. But as happens after a disaster, as the Baltimore Fire receded into the past, interest in poured concrete waned.

One more word about the building: the picture shows the especially graceful semicircular curve of the apse, most notable at the roofline.

University Parkway Bridge, University Parkway and 39th Street, 1908, designed and built by the City Engineer's Department, B. T. Fendall, City Engineer, James A. Paige, Assistant City Engineer, Subdivision of Bridges and New Paving

This reinforced concrete bridge, originally called Stony Run Bridge after the stream it spans, had a somewhat contentious building history in the years 1907 and 1908, judging by the city engineer's reports for those years. The idea for University Parkway was pushed by the Roland Park Company, headed by Edward H. Bouton, as a link between the northwestern suburb and the city's major north-south arteries of Charles, St. Paul, and Calvert streets. Obviously Bouton had an influence over the design of the bridge, for the city engineer's report for 1907 (published January 1908) records that two firms that did a lot of work for Roland Park, landscape architects Olmsted Brothers and architects Wyatt and Nolting, were hired as consultants on the bridge. According to the report, Olmsted Brothers submitted a plan for the "outline of the arch," and Wyatt and Nolting submitted "general outline plans and

details of ornamental work." Also D. B. Banks and F. W. Keyser, consulting engineers, were hired to prepare plans for the reinforced concrete construction. The city initially approved $50,000 for the bridge, but it ended up costing just under $90,000, as the newspapers reported. Mr. Fendall, in the city engineer's report for 1908, appeared to blame the consultants for the overruns, though without naming them, and the wording of the passage makes it unclear whether he found the architectural or the engineering consultants more to blame: "This bridge was not constructed on the plans recommended by me. And while, from an aesthetic point of view, the design as constructed is superior to mine, yet it has cost a great deal more money than the plan proposed by me would have cost. The enormous retaining walls were very expensive and cost much more than the arch."

This is an example of the paramount rule of journalism—Never Assume—in both the usual and a somewhat different from the usual contexts. It is also an example of learning on the job.

Looking at a slide of this photograph, I thought I recognized the bridge as the University Parkway span over Stony Run between 39th and 40th streets, and assumed that the arch was as graceful and beautiful as it is in the photograph. So, based on a long-held but never analyzed assumption, I wrote a text about the beauty of bridges, declaring that this very modest one was a classic example of how bridges tend to be beautiful even when it's obvious that no great expense or design care was lavished upon them. The span under discussion is a concrete structure, not stone, which would be handsomer; and while it has some decorative touches when seen from below, it hardly looks like a bridge when riding on it. It's just a piece of the University Parkway road, with a rise that's virtually imperceptible, and rather clunky walls on either side. But it does have that fine arch shown in the photograph, which sent me into a paean to the beauty of bridges.

I didn't know the date of the bridge, and thought it ought to be included,

and also wanted to make sure that the photograph was indeed of the University Parkway bridge. So I went to the bridge to find easily enough that it was built in 1908, as it declares no fewer than four times, at each end of each flanking wall. To make sure I had the right bridge, I first tried to get close enough to the arch on the San Martin Drive side, but the descent was too steep and the growth too dense to get a good look at the arch. So I went across to the Linkwood Road side, and found to my great surprise that while the bridge looked in some ways like that in the photograph (i.e., the decorative touches), the arch looked far more vertical, and far more awkward. The impression the arch left was so different from that of the picture that upon returning home I threw out the text on the beauty of bridges and wrote another on how photography can alter the appearance of things: that it is not simply a documentary medium, it is a form of art that either can be creative (if one wants to think positively) or can falsify (if one wants to think negatively).

The difference between the arch in the picture and the one I had seen was so pronounced that I called the photographer to make sure his image

was of the University Parkway bridge. He said yes it was, but that he had taken the southern end of the arch, as seen from across the stream from San Martin Drive, where it can be approached through Wyman Park. He also said he had not enhanced the beauty of the arch, the southern end was far handsomer than the northern end which I had seen.

I wasn't sure how that could be true, so I went back and approached the bridge from the south as instructed, to discover that the southern end of the arch is indeed lower, broader, and far lovelier than the northern end, and that the photograph captures rather than creates its beauty.

Thinking back on the sequence of events, I realized that I had done two kinds of assuming. One, the more basic and the cause of most journalistic errors, was the assuming of fact, rather than checking it. After looking at the northern end of the arch I assumed that the southern end looked just like it and that whichever end the photographer had shot he had enhanced the appearance. Hence the piece on the creativity of photographers. Such a piece is valid, but not based on this example. So my false assumption of fact had led to wasted time composing a text that was not valid.

The other kind of assuming, which had led to the earliest form of the text, was the assuming of thought, not the assuming of fact. Upon first looking at the picture of the arch, I was reminded that I have long thought bridges are by their very nature beautiful, and wrote a text to that end without really examining that thought, as indeed I had never done before. Upon examining the thought that bridges are by their very nature beautiful, it became obvious that is not the case. The bridge under discussion, for example, is two-thirds unbeautiful—the roadway with its clunky walls, and the awkward northern end of the arch. Only the southern end of the arch has beauty. Does that make the bridge as a whole beautiful? No. Would you call a person beautiful who had fine eyes but a bulbous nose, a protruding chin, and cauliflower ears?

And surely what's true of the bridge under discussion is true of most bridges. Of course there are beautiful ones, such as the Brooklyn, the Verrazano Narrows, the Golden Gate. But the majority of bridges are merely utilitarian. Think of the bridges over the Jones Falls Expressway. One can say

something for the 29th Street bridge and for the Orleans Street viaduct, but the great majority of them have little or no aesthetic grace, and the green metal thing that carries the light rail to Penn Station is a positive hideosity.

So two kinds of assuming led to two invalid texts, good examples of why Never Assume is the journalist's paramount rule. But there's another kind of lesson here: learning isn't just a process of soaking up knowledge from elsewhere. Thinking for oneself is part of learning. I had assumed for many years that bridges were by their nature beautiful. But I had never really thought about it.

So this has been an example of a good kind of learning: that which combines the process of gaining knowledge (going to the bridge, talking to the photographer, going back to the bridge) with the process of thinking for oneself (analyzing the assumption that bridges are beautiful). Thus we here have a combination of this book's two imperatives: Look again. And think.

Here we have a modest jewel—not a diamond, but not a rhinestone either, maybe a sardonyx or lapis lazuli—left over from almost a century and a half ago, and still standing though it has served no utilitarian purpose for almost a century. A small, stone, classical, pedimented, tempietto-like building, it stands just north of the gate house of the planned community of Cross Keys, in the 5100 block of Falls Road.

It's tiny. To indicate its size, the quoins at the left are the same width as the quoins around the door, and they end at the corner of the building. The near side of this wall is the same width, making the front (this side) and the back of the rectangular building about 12 feet long, with the sides about 20 feet long.

The building faces Falls Road, and the pediment above the front door bears the date 1860 in proud large stone numerals that look as crisp and fresh as when they were new, as do the quoins seen here.

The building's original function was as a valve house for the city's water supply system, the same function as the larger Gothic stone valve house of 1887 in Clifton Park. The designer of that one is not known, but fortunately the almost certain designer of this one is. Though not important architecture, it has good proportions and an appealing overall appearance, if one sees fit to ignore the metal door, which I imagine is a replacement.

The picture was taken at a time of day when the shadows falling across it add to the feeling of age, to the sense of a proud, upright dowager who welcomes her guests with graciousness and dignity.

*900 block West University
Parkway*

This is the Morris Louis Wall. Louis (1912–62), a native of Baltimore and a graduate of the Maryland Institute College of Art, was one of the leading color field painters, along with such artists as Jules Olitski and Kenneth Noland. They were artists in whose works color was the dominant element, so why does this black-and-white photograph of a dirty concrete wall recall Louis?

He used unprimed canvases so that the paint sank into the material, and he poured the paint and manipulated the canvas so that the paint spread across the surface in great veils of color (such as *Blue Veil,* 1958–59) or ran down the surface in rivulets, leaving much of the canvas bare (*Alpha-Iota,* 1961). Either way, the images he produced were characterized by the fluidity of color, with hints of light glimmering here and there.

The wall in this photograph has the same feeling. Ribbons of gray with flickering light appear to roll silkily across the surface, giving the solid concrete the look of a rippling flow of light and shadow, as if a curtain were undulating softly in a gentle breeze. The photograph transforms a hard and grimy object into a symphony of sensuous softness.

Homewood House, North Charles and 34th streets, 1801 and after, Charles Carroll of Homewood, designer

The five-part house is beautifully proportioned and elegantly detailed. Basically it is a one-story house with a high basement and a second floor in the main block. The front façade centers on a formal, vertical portico. Palladian windows flank the hyphen doors, and three variants of the Palladian motif distinguish the front entrance, the garden entrance, and the interior center doorway. The rear, garden façade has a more horizontal porch, and the interior has fine Adamesque decoration.

A Guide to Baltimore Architecture states, of the house's interior architectural decoration, "Through its long life the house, now owned by The Johns Hopkins University, has been used for various purposes including offices, a faculty club, and even a boys' school. Miraculously, it remained virtually intact, so that when finally restored in the 1980s to its former glory, its superb interior architectural detailing did not have to be re-imagined or conjectured, but merely highlighted. It was all there, from the rooms' elegant crown moldings and the hall's vaulted center section to the extraordinary mantels, each one given a different treatment" (1997, pp. 321–22).

This picture captures only a tiny fragment of Homewood House, an internationally admired Federal period country house, but it indicates a considerable portion of what people admire about it. It shows how the sunlight streams through the numerous and generous windows and doors of the principal floor (the house has more than three dozen openings on this floor alone). It shows the beautiful architectural detailing that distinguishes the major rooms, such as the paneled doors, shutters, and wainscoting, and the column, architrave, and cornice that decorate the doorway from the drawing room to the central hall. And it shows elements of the superb restoration that took place in the 1980s, including the period style window and floor treatments, the picking out of architectural details in different colors, and the painted faux marble baseboards. One gets a sense here of why Iain Gale and Richard Bryant, the author and photographer of the book *Living Museums,* which records twenty-six great house museums around the world, chose Homewood as one of the seven included from the Americas. Furthermore, they gave it more pages than any of the other six

(including Mount Vernon), and Gale wrote that it "stands today as one of the most impressive and important Federal buildings in the United States" (*Living Museums,* 1993, p. 10).

The house is a tribute to the man who designed it and had it built, Charles Carroll Jr., now called Charles Carroll of Homewood, son of Charles Carroll of Carrollton, who was the longest-living signer of the Declaration of Independence. It was the father, one of the richest men in America at the time, who paid for it as a wedding gift to his son Charles and his bride Harriet Chew Carroll. Today Homewood House makes Charles Carroll of Homewood widely recognized and respected.

800 block West University Parkway

Photography and writing have a commonality of commonness. They're both so common (in the sense of so general, not in the sense of so inferior) that we take the professional practice of them for granted. Oh, we give due credit to those who are universally recognized as immortals—Stieglitz and Shakespeare, Jane Austen and James Van Der Zee, Proust and Atget. But the professional who's not yet an immortal gets too little credit as an artist because virtually everybody writes and photographs, and tends to think subconsciously, "Oh I could have done that."

Some years ago a friend—I'll call her Josephine—told me a story that perfectly illustrates the attitude. She knew a forty-ish woman who was not famous but made her living as a writer and had had more than one novel published by a New York house. Josephine was also an old friend of the writer's aunt. One day the aunt, paying Josephine a visit, complained that her niece didn't come to see her often enough. In an effort to be diplomatic, Josephine said, "Well, she does work awfully hard."

"Work!" said the aunt. "That girl's never done a day's work in her life. All

she does is sit up in that room of hers and write!"

The story's pertinent to this photograph of a ball and plinth on West University Parkway. Were it not singled out for discussion, probably 99 percent of viewers would give the image a glance, think to themselves, "Oh I could have done that," and pass on. Look again.

At first it appears a simple picture, but the more you look the more there is to notice. Some of it's just there—the bit of moss or lichen that appears to grow on the concrete gives the object a feeling of age and history. But the photograph adds most of the interest.

The placement of the ball and plinth off center gives the composition a dynamic tension, as if there were movement horizontally in one direction or the other. Cutting off the top of the ball and including a tiny triangular sliver of the brick wall that supports this decoration at the bottom of the image gives it a vertical dynamic as well—things are going on beyond the picture frame.

Photographing the ball and plinth from below adds a note of drama—looking up or down at something is always more dramatic than looking flat on. The shadow underneath the ledge has a touch of mystery—you can't see

exactly what's there. The voids on each side of the upright, if looked at as objects, have interesting and complementary shapes: one that of a thin vase and the other that of a fat vase.

In terms of the form, we see a two-dimensional silhouette of the plinth on the left, with a graceful curving arc that descends and meets the top of the ledge just at the left edge of the picture. On the right we see the side as well as the front of the form, giving it three-dimensionality, a sense of volume. The part of the side that we see has a pleasingly curved triangular shape. Again the front edge curves and meets the horizontal of the ledge at picture's edge, making it look more vertical and less extensive than the curve on the left. It isn't, of course; it's a trick played on the eye by the angle of the picture.

Another trick is the way we see the ball in relation to the plinth. The round descending edge appears to meet the plinth near the left front and away from the right rear, making it look off center. It also makes the long exposed top edge of the plinth at right rear balance the more horizontal descending curve on the left, while the short exposed top edge of the plinth at left front balances the more vertical descending curve on the right. As a result, the image as a whole possesses a sense of balance that complements its asymmetry.

In sum, there's a great deal going on—no content, nothing esoteric, no aesthetic theory, in other words, nothing that a viewer has to have specific knowledge to see. Placement of the camera gives a standard architectural ornament significant visual interest and vitality.

This picture is of a staircase at Clifton, the estate of Johns Hopkins where he lived in the summer. He bought it in 1841, with an existing Federal period farmhouse from about 1800. In the early 1850s he had the farmhouse remodeled into an Italianate villa, designed by Niernsee and Neilson, the two most respected architects in Baltimore in the mid-nineteenth century, and that is when this staircase was added.

Hopkins intended to remodel not only the house at Clifton, but also the entire estate, and he did so. He said that he intended to make the estate an earthly paradise. He expanded the estate from 166 acres to about 500 acres, with orchards, gardens, an orangery, an artificial lake with islands and bridges, and a hundred pieces of marble sculpture.

The estate is now a public park, and the house is the only Italianate-style villa left in Baltimore. With members of the Hopkins family taking an interest, it is slowly being restored. Restoration is absolutely the right thing to do, as this staircase can testify. It's both sturdy and handsome, and this light brings out the details, including those of the newel post finial, which in this light looks both solid and delicate.

Clifton, 2701 St. Lo Drive, Clifton Park, ca. 1800, architect unknown; 1852, Niernsee and Neilson, architects

In the early 1850s, Johns Hopkins hired Niernsee and Neilson to remodel a Federal period farmhouse, which he had bought in 1841, into an Italianate villa. The architects added a third floor to the house's main block and extended the wings, an addition on the north side, on the south side a tower with a vaulted porte cochere at the bottom, and also an arcaded porch around the original building. The remodeling was finished by February 1852, when the *Baltimore Sun* wrote that the main entrance under the tower led into "the principal hall, 23 feet high, paved with marble, lighted by four richly stained arched windows, and wainscoted with black walnut, of which the doors and massive stairway are formed" (*A Guide to Baltimore Architecture*, 1997, p. 208). Hopkins died in 1873 with the hope that Clifton would become the location of the university he left money to establish, but the trustees decided otherwise, and in 1895

they sold the Clifton estate to the city for about $722,000, and it became a city park. Most of the time since then, the house has been used as offices and other facilities for the park. Then in 1993 the city turned the building over to Civic Works, Baltimore's youth service corps, and subsequently Civic Works trainees began the restoration with John Brunett as the architect.

I hope Johns Hopkins had a happy life in his mansion on Saratoga Street and in this house on his summer estate Clifton, because his bequest to Baltimore has developed into the most impressive philanthropic accomplishment in the history of Baltimore.

That's saying a lot, because this city has benefited from many philanthropists, beginning with George Peabody and going on to Moses Sheppard, Johns Hopkins, Enoch Pratt, the Walterses, the Garrett family, the Cone sisters, Mary Frick Garrett Jacobs, Jason Epstein, etc.

H. L. Mencken observed, wisely, that the city is the front office of civilization. Baltimore, like many other cities, is a front office of civilization largely because of its philanthropists.

*Walkway, Cathedral Church
of the Incarnation, University
Parkway and St. Paul Street.
For architectural description, see
page 50.*

Death and beauty commingle here.

The image relates in several ways to late modern art, perhaps most obviously to geometric abstraction but more essentially to minimalism. It's a celebration of industrial materials, in this case concrete. It's a demonstration of how the everyday can be turned into art through the artist's vision. The walkway and its walls recall the boxes of Donald Judd. But as a walkway it's closer kin to Carl Andre's compositions of gray metal squares, which the artist put on the floor and invited the public to walk on in contravention of the museum rule that works of art should not be touched. Where this departs from strictest minimalism is in the tonal richness and beauty of its grays, which—especially in terms of the softer modulations of the walkway as opposed to the crisper variations on the walls—give it some relationship to color field painting.

In terms of death, the way the walkway descends and then turns a corner brings to mind the Vietnam War Memorial in Washington—and specifically its flaw. A comparison provides explanation.

The Pinkas Synagogue in Prague has been turned into the most moving of Holocaust memorials, partly because there is nothing graphic or grisly about it—in fact, the opposite. The white-painted walls of its simple, unadorned interior are covered with the names of eighty thousand Jews from Prague and Bohemia killed in concentration camps. They are listed in alphabetical order, each new surname in red, followed by all the first names connected with that surname in black. It has the look of a manuscript, which it is.

Unlike movies or museums, the Pinkas doesn't dramatize. And unlike most memorials, it doesn't symbolize. It is completely devoid of the self-defeating effort to make you feel, which effort, by placing itself between you and the meaning, actually gets in the way. Pinkas is purely a document, a statement of fact, a list of names, austere, quiet, enveloping. Once there, one wants to stay—partly of course because one feels guilty about "going on" as if it were just another stop on a day of sightseeing, which it is. But more deeply because, since there is nothing between you and the meaning, it is a beautiful tribute to those it records, spiritually in its simplicity, and visually as well. Beautiful may seem an inappropriate word, but not if you have been there.

The Vietnam War Memorial, although certainly a fine and moving one, by taking you down and up again—to hell and back—adds symbolism that says, in effect, the record is not enough: we have to do something to it. Those who have been to Pinkas surely know that doing nothing to the record but recording it is a purer and more moving tribute than adding a layer of symbolism.

Putting this walkway in context adds another meaning to the expression "to hell and back." The walkway is at the Episcopal Cathedral of the Incarnation at University Parkway and St. Paul Street. That location makes the walkway's descent below ground stand for Christ's descent into hell after he was crucified.

An interesting question relating to Christianity is whether Jesus knew he was the son of God, and that after his death he would return to life and ascend to heaven. For his life to have the proper meaning for humans, the answer must be no, for he has to have been a human prepared to die for his beliefs without knowing what was coming after. That he was such is the meaning of his last words on the cross according to the evangelists Matthew and Mark: "My God, my God, why hast thou forsaken me?" (Actually a quote from the beginning of Psalm 22.) The utterance of those words indicates that he, like all of us, could not see beyond death. His return to life and ascent to heaven means (if you are a believing Christian) that there is life after death.

In their book *The Testament of Samuel Beckett,* poet Josephine Jacobsen and scholar William Mueller interpret Beckett's play *Waiting for Godot* as taking place on the Saturday between Good Friday and Easter, when humanity doesn't know if Jesus will return to life, and thus prove there is a God and humanity is saved from nothingness after death. This picture, looking only downward, with no horizon and no sky (which represents heaven to those who believe in it) is consonant with the Saturday between Good Friday and Easter in which we all live, with the inability to see beyond death, with the ultimate uncertainty of life.

Death literally, rather than figuratively or symbolically, inhabits this picture in the form of dead leaves, which bring to mind Fall the season, and, because the picture has a religious context, the Fall of Man, which can also be expressed as the death of innocence.

So this image has to do with death in many ways, but beauty occurs and reoccurs, including in relation to death, making it a work in which death and beauty complement one another.

This image of a transit shed at the junction of Charles and St. Paul streets near Overhill Road is a good one with which to end, because it places the viewer at the beginning of an experience. If you think of yourself as standing in the position from which the picture was taken, you are about to proceed along the paved walkway, to enter the little Arts-and-Crafts-looking building, perhaps to explore it a bit, and to emerge on the other side.

In other words you are about to have an experience that will remain in your memory for whatever use you may wish to put it to in the future, which is what we hope this book is about. All books are about that to one degree or another, but this one has the specific didactic purpose of promoting the combination of visual exploration and thought.

This picture, because it puts you in the position of looking ahead, also brings to mind baseball player Satchel Paige's oft-quoted rule of life, "Never look back; something might be gaining on you." He didn't mean it literally in a physical sense, of course. He meant it figuratively, and the something he had in mind was no doubt death, about which there is no "might." What his rule advises people to do is to live in

Transit shed, St. Paul Street at Charles Street, near Overhill Road

the present and look toward the future, don't live in the past, for that can only bring regrets and sadness.

It is a lesson I learned more deeply from my mother than from Satchel Paige's rule. Even when she was in her nineties (she died three weeks short of her ninety-sixth birthday) she never reminisced, she never longed for the past, she never waxed nostalgic. Or if such thoughts entered her mind she never uttered them. She always wanted to learn what others were doing with their lives and looking forward to, she always wanted to plan ahead, she always liked having a project, whether a book, something to sew, someplace to go, a decision to make, a way to be of help to someone. It was always, "What's going on at the paper?" "Come on out to dinner and I'll get up a bridge game." "Let's discuss the election, I want to figure out who I'm going to vote for." Her favorite cause was the environment, and one of the last checks she wrote was to the Chesapeake Bay Foundation, whose hopes and plans she knew would not come to fruition until many years after she died, if ever.

She would have liked this picture. But she wouldn't have liked that last paragraph. I was looking back.

Photowalks

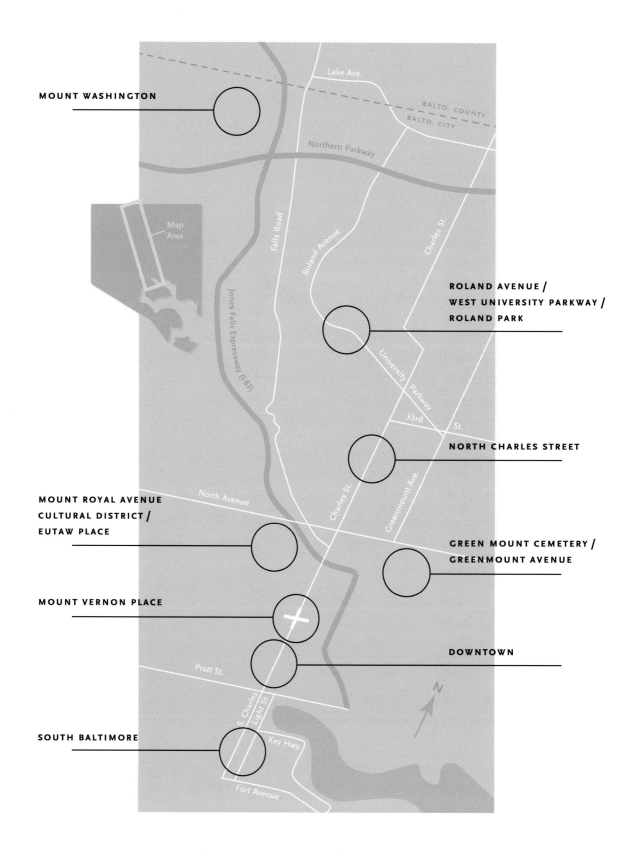

MOUNT WASHINGTON

ROLAND AVENUE /
WEST UNIVERSITY PARKWAY /
ROLAND PARK

NORTH CHARLES STREET

MOUNT ROYAL AVENUE
CULTURAL DISTRICT /
EUTAW PLACE

GREEN MOUNT CEMETERY /
GREENMOUNT AVENUE

MOUNT VERNON PLACE

DOWNTOWN

SOUTH BALTIMORE

Lake Ave.

BALTO. COUNTY
BALTO. CITY

Northern Parkway

Map
Area

Falls Road

Roland Avenue

Charles St.

Jones Falls Expressway (I-83)

University Parkway

33rd St.

North Avenue

Charles St.

Greenmount Ave.

Pratt St.

S. Charles

Light St.

Key Hwy.

Fort Avenue

N

JOHN DORSEY

JAMES DUSEL

Retired art critic of the *Baltimore Sun*, Dorsey has written and lectured extensively and curated several exhibitions on art and architecture.

A secondary school teacher of Latin and photography in Baltimore, DuSel has exhibited his photographs of the built environment in galleries in the United States and Brazil.